DESIGNING HOPE

VISIONS TO SHAPE OUR FUTURE

by

SARAH HOUSLEY

When did we stop dreaming of a better future?

What happened to the sci-fi golden age of the 1950s, when futurism flourished as a discipline and drove innovation?

In these times of climate breakdown, war and widening inequality we either struggle to imagine something good for the times to come or we fail to picture any future at all. The exciting outcomes we dreamed of, from the space race to the wonder material plastic, have brought contingent problems of their own. We haven't yet developed mainstream and accessible new narratives to replace these failures, and if you ask someone to imagine 'the future', they'll probably still picture flying cars.

Designing Hope resets expectations. Through the lens of four emerging futures – More-than-human, Degrowth, Solarpunk and the Metaverse – Sarah Housley shows us visions of hope that inspire action and critical thinking about how we'll live in the decades to come.

© Claire Dickinson

SARAH HOUSLEY is a design futurist and trend forecaster, and the former Head of Consumer Tech at WGSN. She has consulted for numerous brands on topics ranging from the future of water to our future relationships with robots, and spoken internationally at events including London Design Festival, iF Chengdu, and Dutch Design Week.

She has contributed to BBC Radio 4, as well as print and digital media including *The Financial Times*, *The Guardian*, *British Vogue* and *Stylist* magazine. She teaches Futures and Innovation at the London College of Fashion.

THE
INDIGO
PRESS

DESIGNING HOPE

VISIONS TO SHAPE OUR FUTURE

SARAH HOUSLEY

THE
INDIGO
PRESS

THE INDIGO PRESS
50 Albemarle Street
London W1S 4BD
www.theindigopress.com

The Indigo Press Publishing Limited Reg. No. 10995574
Registered Office: Wellesley House, Duke of Wellington Avenue
Royal Arsenal, London SE18 6SS

COPYRIGHT © SARAH HOUSLEY 2025

First published in Great Britain in 2025 by The Indigo Press

Sarah Housley asserts the moral right to be identified as the author of this work in accordance with the Copyright, Designs and Patents Act 1988

A CIP catalogue record for this book is available from the British Library

ISBN: 978-1-911648-97-0
eBook ISBN: 978-1-911648-98-7

All rights reserved. No part of this publication may be reproduced, stored in a retrieval system or transmitted, in any form or by any means, electronic, mechanical, photocopying, recording or otherwise, without the prior permission of the publishers.

Cover design © Luke Bird
Artwork © Víctor Arce: www.executabledreams.net
Art direction by House of Thought
Typeset by Tetragon, London
Printed and bound by CPI (UK) Ltd, Croydon CR0 4YY

EU GPSR Authorised Representative:
LOGOS EUROPE, 9 rue Nicolas Poussin, 17000, LA ROCHELLE, France
E-mail: Contact@logoseurope.eu

1 3 5 7 9 8 6 4 2

Contents

An Introduction to Futures 9

1 MORE-THAN-HUMAN 27
   Cross-Species Empathy 35
   Designing Symbiosis 40
   Rewilding Worlds 47
   Gardening Your World View 54

2 DEGROWTH 61
   Designing Transitions 70
   Less Meaning More 76
   Localism and Communalism 82
   Low-Carbon Transport 88

3 SOLARPUNK 97
   DIY Networks 105
   Solarised Thinking 111
   Radical Nature 118
   Joyful Alternatives 125

4 METAVERSE	131
Hype Cycle Futures	138
Reality Privilege	144
Co-Created Worlds	149
The Natureverse	155

Call to Action: How to Think into Futures –
Tools and Thought-Starters — 161

Notes — 171
Bibliography — 183
Acknowledgements — 187

An Introduction to Futures

People are not excited about the future any more. We live in a time of unrelenting polycrisis, which makes today feel more urgent than tomorrow. When we do turn our minds to what's next, our established images of the future – most of them made or popularised at least 70 years ago – are creaking with age. Much of what we've been looking ahead to for the past century or more has arrived, certainly from a technological standpoint: we have pocket computers, worldwide digital connectivity, convincingly intelligent AI and even self-driving cars. Now, we face a significant problem: we're lacking new futures to pin our hopes to. And that has major repercussions on our ability to improve the systems we live within today, as well as on our chances of creating better futures for both ourselves and the generations who will follow.

Science fiction is not really about seeing the future; it's about more clearly seeing the present. And for a while now, science-fiction writers have been telling us that something is wrong. Speaking at a Long Now seminar in 2004, author Bruce Sterling noted that 'the loss of the future is becoming acute... People need a motivating vision of what comes next and the awareness that more will happen after that, that the future is a process not a destination.'[1] In an interview on BBC Radio 4's *Today* programme in 2020, author William Gibson spoke of 'future fatigue' and how it was contributing to a lack of visions of the next century. Where the 20th century was richly populated with stories and images about the 21st century, he pointed out, we rarely (if ever) mention the 22nd century.[2]

Alongside this future fatigue, when people do think about the future, there is a growing sense of pessimism about what is likely to happen next. In the shorter term, a 2021 poll by the McCourtney Institute for Democracy at Penn State University found that 84% of Americans described themselves as 'extremely worried' or 'very worried' about the country's future over the next 12 months and 22% said that nothing makes them hopeful.[3] Taking a longer view of future mindsets, a 2022 poll by YouGov found that the percentage of British people who believe that humans will never become extinct has dropped by seven percentage points (from 30% to 23%) since 2016.[4]

It has been said that every generation thinks it will be the last – but this generation is remarkable for having more reason than most to think so. Alongside an unstable geopolitical landscape, there is a creeping sense of climate anxiety – across all generations, but particularly younger ones – as the day-to-day impacts of multiple environmental crises start to play out more noticeably. In a 2021 survey of 10,000 young people aged 16–25 from 10 countries on attitudes to climate change, 75% said that they think the future is frightening and 55% agreed with the statement 'humanity is doomed'.[5]

Essayist Rebecca Solnit has attributed today's 'apocalyptic thinking' to a 'narrative failure: the inability to imagine a world different than the one we currently inhabit'.[6] Scientist and imagination activist Phoebe Tickell has written that we are in 'a period of story breakdown', which she further describes as 'a chasm between stories that used to function and new stories which haven't yet gathered enough coherence to function effectively'.[7] Environmentalist and climate activist Bill McKibben has summarised what we need as 'a world worth wanting'.[8]

Humans have dreamed of the future for as long as we know. Throughout history, cultures and societies have featured shamans, oracles and prophets. Psychologists have defined prospection (the representation of possible futures) as 'a core organising principle of animal and human behaviour',[9] and studies have indicated that humans have a 'fundamental and universal bias' to imagine how things could be better than they currently are.[10] Futures are present throughout history, but the 20th century saw an inflection point as an institutionalised practice of future forecasting and futures studies emerged, based on technological innovation and linear, continuous economic growth.

After the Second World War, it became an increasingly prevalent mindset – in industrialised, Western and prosperous countries at least – to be excited about the future. The golden age of futurism traces back to the 1950s, when science fiction flourished and a brighter future seemed assured. In the early 20th century, governments had begun to form planning and research committees to influence state strategy and policymaking. In the post-war innovation boom, research institutes and forecasters were able to claim new positions of power as research and development (R&D) became a focus, particularly for the US, which was investing heavily in achieving technological superiority across space tech and defence.

RAND, the California-based think tank, began in 1946 as Project RAND, which researched military futures and published a concept study for a spaceship that would function as a satellite. By the 1960s, it was extending its approach to futures R&D beyond military and defence to the education and healthcare sectors. Meanwhile, the Defense Advanced Research Projects Agency (DARPA) was founded in 1958 to help the US accelerate its rate of technological innovation and win the space race. Its first three pillars of research were space technology, ballistic missile defence and solid propellants. It went on to develop rockets, satellites and unmanned vehicles and achieve breakthroughs in materials science and firsts in computing, including the first mouse and the cognitive computing systems that became the voice assistant Siri.

Numerous research institutes and think tanks have played important roles globally since then to shape our images of the future, including the World Future Society, founded in 1966, and the Copenhagen Institute for Futures Studies, founded in 1969. However, the predominant model for corporate and national futurism remains rooted in economic growth, leaps forward in technology, and military benefit.

With forecasting established in political, military and economic uses, it extended across the corporate world in the form of foresight and trend forecasting. By the 1970s, corporate strategy was using techniques such as scenario forecasting: significant practitioners included Royal Dutch Shell. Companies and brands increasingly built forecasting into their budgets to make sure that the things they were designing and making – ad campaigns, product ranges, brand strategy – would fit with the needs, moods and priorities of the people who would be buying from them in a few years' time. Trend forecasting in particular boomed in the 2000s as 'lifestyle' became a buzzword and people started to define themselves more by the products they bought. The dawn of social media made trends more visible and more popular with consumers, and trend cycles became shorter and more disposable as people moved on to the next big thing.

Then, things changed. The year 2016 marked a shift to a markedly less stable geopolitical landscape. At the same time, climate breakdown started to ramp up, and social justice issues moved into the mainstream cultural spotlight. The future felt more urgent but less knowable. Trend forecasting became more important to companies – because they needed to plan ahead with greater accuracy – but the work itself became more difficult as global macro trends became ever more volatile, uncertain, complex and ambiguous (VUCA).

The global onset of the Covid-19 pandemic in 2020 brought with it another pivotal moment in futures thinking. One of the effects of the pandemic was to open the Overton window – the window of political possibility for action or change that the general public consider acceptable, as coined by American policy analyst Joseph Overton in the 1990s. The multiple, immediate changes that the pandemic necessitated also brought about a mass questioning of our 'consensus futures' – the ideas about the future that people across a society all basically agree on and have cast as 'the future' in the popular imagination.

The accelerated scientific innovation and implementation that occurred during the pandemic, with vaccines created and rolled out in record time and on a huge scale, showed how quickly institutional change could happen when it was considered a priority. From a social and behavioural point of view, government and public health responses to the spread of the virus changed everything from how we behaved in public spaces and with friends and family to whether we were allowed to leave the house, and how long for. Significant longer-term social and cultural shifts also happened much more quickly due to the pandemic and the lockdowns it brought about, including rises in gaming, working from home, and e-commerce and a permanent shift to cashless and contactless transactions.

This living proof of how quickly our systems and behaviour could change when needed – if backed by a strong incentive and a political will – made many people hope that we could change other aspects of the way we lived. And while many of the other second-order effects of the pandemic were short-lived, this hope is ongoing.

The writer, educator and activist Donella H. Meadows once noted that 'vision is not only missing almost entirely from policy discussions; it is missing from our culture. We talk about our fears, frustrations and doubts endlessly, but we talk only rarely and with embarrassment about our dreams.'[11] In our current time, vision is crucial and must be placed front and centre in our culture.

The years ahead hold the potential to be a galvanising time: with the Overton window opened and new ideas seeming possible, it's time to start creating the futures we want to bring into being.

The futures thinking of the 2020s is necessarily evolving to be different to that which came before it. Modern futures thinking aims to be inclusive and expansive and to bring in diverse and varied viewpoints and needs. To do this, futures thinking and forecasting need to be four things: plural, preferred, protopian and participatory.

PLURAL

Words have a powerful ability to shape and set our thinking. Using the plural 'futures' instead of the singular 'future' helps to cultivate the mindset that there is not one set future but many possible futures. These futures will be different for every single person and will markedly differ according to where that person lives; their financial circumstances, gender identity, race and cultural heritage; and many more factors.

Using the plural 'futures' also reminds us that there are multiple perspectives on the future, and that more diverse lenses and experiences will create inherently different futures visions. The history of institutionalised futures thinking is heavily Western, white, colonial and male. The industry has acknowledged its WEIRD bias, borrowing an acronym from behavioural psychology that refers to the disproportionate study of and attention paid to Western, educated, industrialised, rich and democratic people and countries. That bias is slowly being addressed as different global futurisms, most notably Afrofuturism, become increasingly influential, but much more needs to be done to make futures practice more inclusive, diverse and expansive.

Taking a plural approach to futures can encourage us to think about multiple futures that expand, coexist, interconnect and flow between one another, rather than thinking about only one rigid, universal future that sits neatly inside of existing systems. This approach opens up possibilities and fosters a greater diversity of perspectives and thinking.

PREFERRED

As we consider what is possible, we can simultaneously think about which futures would be preferred. Continuing the mindset that futures are plural and can be shaped, it is important to develop a point of view on which futures you want. When one homogeneous future – a single future – is presented over and over again, and sold to you as the only choice, it can start to feel set in stone and therefore difficult to question or critique. It's useful to remember that no one future is inevitable. Developing preferred futures may mean rejecting the consensus future or adapting it to your needs.

Future visions are frequently rejected, particularly when they are developed and promoted almost exclusively by a narrow group of people with a vested interest in making them happen. Once these narrow futures are socialised (made more widely known), they may hold little appeal to a general public who don't see the need or benefit of them. A high-profile example was the introduction of Google Glass, the smart glasses that were heavily hyped by their makers and initial users on their launch in 2013. Presented as an exciting and inevitable future vision of ubiquitous computing, which had long been a dream for the tech industry, they were quickly rejected by wider society, with some early users described as 'glassholes'. Staying true to a preferred future may mean rejecting techno-optimist futures, or at least critiquing them – a theme we'll continue to explore throughout this book.

With preferred futures, one key question to ask is 'preferred by whom, and for whom?' In this way, you can get an idea of who would benefit from this future and how – usually by gaining money and power – and conversely, who wouldn't benefit and would be likely to experience greater inequity or oppression. There is a long history of technological innovations that have excluded, othered or purposefully targeted marginalised groups, including women; Black, Indigenous and People of Colour (BIPOC) communities; LGBTQIA+ communities; and people with disabilities. This history is increasingly being called out by activists and scholars, including Ruha Benjamin, author of *Race After Technology: Abolitionist Tools for the New Jim Code*,[12] and Caroline Criado Perez, author of *Invisible Women*[13] – but more needs to be done by futures thinkers to interrogate how futures are being designed and whom they are being designed by and for.

PROTOPIAN

We need to start framing futures beyond the utopian/dystopian binary. Utopia is impossible by definition – the word means 'no place' – and dystopias, while alluring, are not motivating. This binary is so ingrained in our thinking that it has become mundane, clichéd, and therefore dangerous: it is preventing progress and stopping us from imagining more varied and original futures.

Both concepts are entrenched in tropes and stereotypes. These images of the future feel familiar and even safe – however unappealing they would be to live in – simply because we've seen them so much. They dominate TV, film and literature and feature in adverts and marketing campaigns, particularly for consumer tech products and services. Because we have grown up consuming them, they can feel inevitable, and their familiarity has made them limiting and uninspiring.

Protopia is a useful alternative framing to the utopia/dystopia binary. Kevin Kelly, a technology writer and the founding executive editor of *WIRED* magazine, defines protopia as 'a state that is better today than yesterday, although it might be only a little better'.[14] This definition recognises that incremental change is still change and that futures need to be progressing continuously. A protopian future that is emerging and an improvement on the past but not perfect is more useful than a perfect future vision that remains far-off and never materialises.

Monika Bielskyte, founder of the Protopia Futures framework, offers an alternative view of protopia as 'proactive prototyping of radically hopeful and inclusive futures that shifts the gaze from technological panaceas to focus on future cultural values and social ethics'.[15] This definition rejects the idea that only technology drives futures, and brings people firmly back into the picture. Both definitions usefully expand the futures framework beyond the idea of one future – utopia or dystopia, good or bad – to something far more interesting, inspiring and achievable.

Since Kevin Kelly introduced the idea of protopia in 2011, this in-between space – of radical hope and inclusion, where our futures are not perfect but are also not doomed – has grown more present across creative culture. In science-fiction literature, protopias are flourishing. Kim Stanley Robinson's novels present a protopian take on tackling climate change, particularly his 2020 novel, *The Ministry for the Future*. Becky Chambers' science-fiction novels depict postcolonial civilisations practising happy, radical inclusion across genders, species and planets. Both are well worth reading to bring fresh thinking about liveable and hopeful futures into your orbit.

PARTICIPATORY

The more people who participate equally in futures thinking and futures designing, the more inclusive and representative these futures are likely to become. To this end, futures practice should be open to all, not cordoned off as a specialised area that you have to be an expert in to engage in. Critical futures thinking – being aware of the futures that are being presented to you, evaluating them, and designing and building your own futures – is an important supplementary skill that all creatives, professionals and citizens should have and use.

UNESCO, the United Nations' global laboratory of ideas, has designated 'futures literacy' as an essential competency for the 21st century, defining it as 'the competency that allows people to better understand the role of the future in what they see and do'.[16] Futures literacy confers power: if you can imagine the future – and have access to the space, mental bandwidth and tools to do so – you can start to shape it.

As well as opening up futures thinking to higher-education students (across many subjects, rather than being siloed in design and other creative subjects), learning institutions are starting to integrate futures practices into both school-level education and lifelong learning opportunities. Teach The Future Denmark, an initiative from the Copenhagen Institute for Futures Studies, open-sources its teaching material for teachers to use in their classrooms. The aim is to give young people the skills and confidence to think about the future and start to envision and create it themselves.

Making futures more accessible will mean going beyond the typical tools of whiteboard ideation sessions and lots of Post-it notes to enable different types of learning, including more experiential and hands-on ways of thinking about futures. Design fiction is one of these: this method involves creating objects from possible futures that people can hold, feel, use and think about in a more physical way. Experiential futures is another: this branch of futures immerses people in future spaces and scenarios that can be explored, felt, embodied and interacted with, similarly to immersive art or theatre, to bring future concepts to life in physical and memorable ways. Both techniques present thinking about the future as an expressive and creative process, something that can spark the imagination and open up more possibilities.

This book outlines four futures. All four are possible. They present hope, and they offer challenges. They might make the world more equal in some ways; they might also make existing inequalities and injustices worse, and introduce new ones. The four futures here overlap: two, three or four could coexist, and elements from all of them may well mingle and mix together in the one future you eventually inhabit. They all present new ideas about society, communities, how to develop and use technology, and how our economies should be designed; they all include old ideas, too. No single 'future' is good or bad – this is too simplistic, and it won't help us to think that way – and ultimately no one future will come true.

My background is in trend forecasting, which is a type of futures practice that focuses on tracking new ideas and making them tangible, practical and commercial. I trained in design, and the area of futures I work in is design futures. To me, this means thinking about the kinds of objects, experiences, spaces and systems we'll need and want in the future, and how best to make and use them. Designers are often natural futurists, because they tend to be curious and imaginative people who enjoy thinking about different possibilities and joining the dots between ideas. But as well as being fun, this is an important part of the job: anything that is designed is new to the world, and because it doesn't exist yet, it needs to be appropriate for the future in which it will exist. Futures thinking is crucial in design because it helps us to consider the long-term ethical implications of what we make and anticipate unintended consequences.

Broadly speaking, futures thinking can be focused anywhere from five to fifty years or more into the future. It can be local or global in its focus, and it can be generalised across society or made highly specific to one community, industry or organisation.

People who work in futures get asked two main questions when they explain their job to someone: what have you predicted right, and what's coming next? The pedantic answer is that futurists develop projections, not predictions, and these are highly variable, so it's not a simple exercise to look back and see what we 'got right' – but we can see where an idea succeeded, or where its trajectory curved or stalled in ways that weren't anticipated. The longer you work in futures thinking, the more examples there are to draw on. As my career has progressed, I've seen many of the radical ideas that were once emerging become more established and normalised. Two examples are lab-grown meat and mycelium leather, which fit within a larger macro trend towards biodesign and have both moved over the past decade from being niche research concepts to real products that are on sale. I've worked with companies over the past 15 years to anticipate and prepare for water scarcity and to think about how human relationships with intelligent machines are going to evolve. Both topics have only become more important in the years since those workshops.

The futures we will explore in this book are all emerging today as influential ideas and are all being invested in by private companies, governments and NGOs. In this sense, they are all 'real' futures.

I've tried to bring each future to life with real examples that are being lived in or designed today;

I encourage you to look up and seek out the ideas, movements and products that stand out to you, with the caveat that not every example will remain valid or static. I've also included further speculations about what might happen next. As you read through the futures, I invite you to imagine living within them. What would you like, and what would you want to change or adapt? What would be fair, unfair or unevenly accessible? How might oppression or inequity be present in these futures? What would need to change in our current systems and society for these futures to come to be?

At the end of the book, after the four futures, I'll leave you with some questions and methods of evaluation that can be used to think further into each future vision – or other future visions of your own choosing and design. I encourage you to use this book as a jumping-off point. Each one of us should have the power to shape, influence and critique the future – and we should all be using this power.

I

More-Than-Human

'So: nature? You are nature, nature is you. Natural is what happens. The word is useless as a divide, there is no Human apart from Nature, you have no thoughts or feelings without your body, and the Earth is your body, so please dispense with that dichotomy of human/nature, and attend to your own health, which is to say your biosphere's health.'

Science-fiction author Kim Stanley Robinson,
from an interview in *Farsight* in 2022[1]

More-than-human is a mindset that holds that species and intelligences other than humans inhabit this planet – plants, animals, microorganisms and more – and that their needs and perspectives matter and should be taken into account in the ways we run our societies and inhabit our environments. The term 'more-than-human' was introduced by ecologist and philosopher David Abram in his 1996 book, *The Spell of the Sensuous: Perception and Language in a More-Than-Human World*, which put forward a thesis of how disconnected the human body had become from the rest of the natural world, and proposed that we live as part of it. More-than-human thinking is no more, and no less, radical than that. If you start probing into the idea, though, you soon see that really taking on this world view and implementing it at scale will entail reorganising most of our prevalent infrastructures and societal systems.

The viewpoint that non-human lifeforms are intelligent and even sentient – that they have thoughts, feelings and distinct personalities – is increasingly widely held by scientists. Research on animal intelligence is building year on year, with the sentience of more animals and wider categories of species being recognised and appreciated: see the octopus's use of tools, parental care, and ability to recognise faces of other species of animal, or the recently discovered ability of bees – like birds, primates and dolphins – to understand the concept of zero. These 'other intelligences' are increasingly being understood and respected on their own terms, for their own uniqueness. An octopus's brain extends into its tentacles, giving it an embodied intelligence; a spider stores information in its webs, extending intelligence outside of the body. Alongside intelligences, animal senses and perception are increasingly being studied: in his 2022 book, *An Immense World*, writer Ed Yong takes an enthusiastic and imaginative tour of non-human perception, including electric fish, sonar-sensing bats and canine scent, to expand the human lens into a more-than-human sensory feast.

There has been a similar rise in research into plants and trees to unearth in much more detail how they connect and cooperate in cross-species communities. Trees communicate with one another using rooted mycelium networks, creating a 'wood wide web', in which they support each other in times of need. Their branches leave a gap – a phenomenon called crown shyness – allowing their neighbours' canopies to also reach the sky. Plants have recently been found to engage in acoustic interaction, high-frequency crackling sounds that occur when they are stressed and are thought to be used to convey information to nearby animals or other plants.

Even the smallest organisms have been found to have some form of experience or perception. Slime mould, single-celled organisms that lack brains, can make decisions and optimise their routes more efficiently than the smartest supercomputers humans have ever made. Mitochondria – the subcellular organelles that are present in most cells – can communicate with each other and synchronise behaviours.

We're also increasingly aware that people are made up of multiple organisms – we are home to archaea, fungi, viruses and other microbes, and our microbiomes balance microbial cells to human cells at a ratio of 1.3:1, or 39 trillion to 30 trillion, making each of us distinctly more-than-human in our own right.[2]

As our idea of intelligence expands, our understanding of who and what should have rights is changing. For example, most countries recognise corporations as having legal personhood, giving them rights such as property ownership. Increasingly, laws are being brought into discussion that would give natural entities such as rivers a similar status. New Zealand's Whanganui River was granted legal personhood in 2017 following extensive work by Māori activists;[3] the Mutuhekau Shipu River in Canada was granted legal personhood in 2021 and now has nine rights, including the right to flow and be pollution-free.[4] The Amazon has had legal rights since 2018, following a ruling by Colombia's Supreme Court in response to a case brought against the Colombian government by 25 young people aged 7 to 25.[5]

Around the world, more rivers, as well as lakes and forests, have been recognised as having legal rights, and the momentum continues. Campaigners in the UK have called for mature trees, which contribute significantly to biodiversity, to be protected in a similar way to historic buildings. In Italy, 22,000 trees are classified as national monuments,[6] and there is hope that this will set a precedent.

In the UK, the Animal Welfare (Sentience) Act, passed in 2022, recognises animal sentience in law and covers all vertebrates and some invertebrates, including lobsters and octopuses;[7] similar measures have been passed in Spain and New Zealand and are being explored in other countries. In France, the government adopted ecocide laws in 2021 that make it possible to prosecute people for offences committed against nature;[8] Belgium implemented ecocide laws at international level in 2024.[9] Activists are now pushing for ecocide to be recognised in EU laws, as well as in the International Criminal Court, which tries individuals for crimes against humanity. Active in more than 50 countries, the organisation ClientEarth uses the law to fight global environmental challenges, defend wildlife and habitats, and protect forests.

Ecopsychologist Pella Thiel is developing a Rights of Nature framework, which she aims to see installed on a global scale alongside the Declaration of Human Rights. 'As there is no human health, indeed no human life, without Nature, human rights are meaningless if the rest of nature is right-less,' she writes.[10]

The more-than-human mindset has its spiritual and cultural roots in numerous long-standing cultures and world views, including panpsychism (the idea that everything contains consciousness) and animism (the belief that all things have a spirit, or that nature holds power over people). For countries in the Global North, this marks a major shift from the mechanistic world view that has become dominant, but for many cultures, more-than-human thinking and language have remained ingrained throughout history.

The more-than-human focus on relational perspectives, interdependence and ecological thinking draws deeply from traditional Indigenous knowledge and belief systems. Indigenous Amazon climate activist Samela Sateré Mawé explained, in an interview by the Mongabay news portal in 2022: 'When we say that the future is ancestral, we are trying to make people turn inward, turn toward their inner selves and see that we are also the forest, we are also the planet and that we are part of the Earth. And that we are the future and that this is completely connected to our past, our ancestors, because when we understand ourselves as part of a biome, part of an ecosystem and as part of a whole, we will not degrade.'[11] Indigenous scholar Enrique Salmón coined the term 'kincentric ecology' to describe similar world views.[12]

Indigenous communities around the world have long histories of environmental stewardship, and as more-than-human futures gain support, this wealth of lived experience is being recognised as vital in preventing climate breakdown and restoring nature. According to the UN, Indigenous peoples steward over 80% of the planet's remaining biodiversity. The strong presence of Indigenous knowledge experts at Glasgow's COP26 climate conference in 2021 was seen as a key achievement for the event, where leaders from 145 countries pledged US$1.7 billion to reverse deforestation and land degradation by 2030. In a more-than-human future, Indigenous communities will have a key role to play in shaping mainstream understanding of the relationship dynamic with nature that needs to be cultivated.

Coupled with the climate crisis is the nature crisis – the loss of animal life and health that humans have caused, resulting in biodiversity loss. We have created and are living through the sixth mass extinction, in which species are dying out at a rate 1,000–10,000 times higher than it would be without human impact. (The last mass extinction event occurred 66 million years ago and killed off 78% of species, including dinosaurs). The current extinction event is starkly visible to many people through the 'windscreen phenomenon' – the observation that dead bugs accumulate in much lower numbers on car windscreens now than they used to, as insect populations have declined so drastically over the past few decades. A 2017 study conducted in Germany found a 75% decrease in total flying insect biomass over 27 years.[13] The problem, of course, extends far beyond insects. Wildlife populations decreased by 69% globally between 1970 and 2022. A 2023 study found that 94% of the global biomass of mammals now comprises humans and our livestock; only 6% is made up of wild mammals.[14]

The probable zoonotic origin of the Covid-19 pandemic has only made the nature crisis clearer. As animals are pushed into new spaces by human encroachment and climate breakdown, or have their habitats taken away and not replaced, we create the circumstances for viruses and diseases to spread more quickly between species that may previously not have mixed or interacted in such close proximity. In the aftermath of the pandemic, the spread of avian flu has continued to make this point.

In short: we can see the problem, we can sense it, and we can also sense how our behaviour needs to shift. The way we think about the lifeforms and environments we share the world with directly affects how we treat them, and how we see our own role within that world. In an age of climate breakdown, a change in thinking here could be transformative. The outcome of this shift in mindset would be to treat other natural entities with respect, to see humans as nature, and to move from extractive, control-based relationships with other parts of nature to balanced, regenerative and reciprocal relationships. The more we discover about how other lifeforms live, feel and communicate, the more we tend to empathise with them.

CROSS-SPECIES EMPATHY

An increasing number of cultural and creative initiatives are compelling us to spend time understanding how other lifeforms might be thinking and feeling, and the most interesting are engaging with the concept of deep ecology – the belief that nature has inherent value, rather than being solely or primarily a useful resource for humans.

Immersive art installations are drawing on the unique power of art to have a visceral effect on us – to make us feel the value of nature as well as understand information about climate breakdown. Es Devlin's *Conference of the Trees* installation at Glasgow's COP26 climate conference placed speakers and attendees literally within nature, positioning a stage and seating amongst 197 trees and plants so that the attendees had to physically sit with and experience the very thing they were debating the merits of supporting. The installation aimed to emphasise the weight of responsibility that humans bear as we make decisions that will drastically affect the future of all life on the planet. 'I wanted to view the conference of the parties from the perspective of a non-human species bearing witness to the decisions the humans might make,' Devlin has said of the installation.[15]

Artist Olafur Eliasson has similarly been putting nature directly into people's cultural experience. His site-specific *Life* installation at Fondation Beyeler in Switzerland extended the pond from the gardens outside into the gallery to make plants, algae and water into viewers as well as artworks. The aim was to emphasise the coexistence of everyone involved in the exhibition, human and non-human.

Eliasson previously installed 30 icebergs, imported from Greenland, outside Tate Modern in London to bring a physical, melting reminder of the reality of the climate crisis to passers-by. He described that artwork as 'a very tangible encounter with the consequences of actions… I really hope that *Ice Watch* can create feelings of proximity and presence, and make us engage.'[16]

In the age of Zoom, digital versions of these experiences are also possible. As the European Green Capital of 2021, the Finnish city of Lahti created Lahti Green Screen, a camera link to a local forest and lake that could be dialled in to meetings to have a seat at the table. Civic employees could choose to have the view on-screen as a participant during teleconference meetings – again bearing witness to their actions.

In April 2022, Nieuwe Instituut in Rotterdam converted itself into a zoöp, a structure of decision-making that considers and protects the interests of non-human life. It has appointed to its board a representative for the voices of non-human life, or a speaker for the living, the first of whom is landscape architect Maike van Stiphout. The institute's general and artistic director Aric Chen describes the intent as 'not... just humans trying to do things at our convenience that are better, but actually giving agency to non-human entities'.[17]

There has been a significant uptick in recent years in immersive experiences that promote interspecies empathy, giving humans the perspectives of other lifeforms. Several of these use gaming as their medium: *Sharing Prosperity* is an interactive game experience created by digital studio DVTK in collaboration with social anthropologist Professor Henrietta L. Moore, who is the director of the Institute for Global Prosperity at UCL. The game was designed to encourage a relational economy of wealth-sharing between species, inviting players to take the role of a rock, waterfall or mushroom. Other games promote post-human, interspecies prosperity. In *Timberborn*, released in 2021, players are tasked with rebuilding a city as part of an ingenious beaver colony who are living in the ruins of a long-gone human society.

Digital art collective Marshmallow Laser Feast's *Sanctuary of the Unseen Forest* (2022) is one of a number of recent video installations aiming to bring the inner workings of trees and forests to life for a human audience. Set inside a *Ceiba pentandra* tree in the Amazon rainforest, the video shows the tree absorbing nutrients through its roots and performing photosynthesis.

One of the interactive art highlights at the SXSW tech festival in 2023 was *Symbiosis*, a multisensory virtual reality (VR) experience by Polymorf and Studio Biarritz, in which viewers could choose to be a toad, a slime mould, a butterfly–human hybrid or an AI. In the multi-user experience, each role interconnects, emphasising nature's shared and interdependent ecosystems. The festival also played host to *Forager*, an art experience by Winslow Porter and Elie Zananiri, which puts people into the life cycle of a mushroom, growing from an aerial spore to part of a mycelium network.

Also using speculative fiction, Finsbury Park in London hosted an interspecies festival from 2020 to 2025, in which participants of an immersive fiction – called *The Treaty of Finsbury Park* – were assigned a species to role-play. Adopting the eyes, ears and priorities of their mentor species – a dog, bee, Canada goose, stag beetle, grass plant, squirrel or plane tree – participants could join a multispecies choir and co-create a new interspecies treaty for the park to adopt.

Artists and makers are also starting to collaborate directly with other parts of nature to create performances and dialogues. Love Hultén's custom-built musical instrument, Desert Songs, translates the biofeedback produced by cacti into notes. The cacti's electrical variations are analysed by a PlantWave device, then processed by a stomp box and a synth. The cacti's performance is also visualised on the outside of the device.

These experiences, while creatively extending the human world view, are arguably limited by still being based on human assumptions, preferences and aesthetic expectations. In many of the games, experiences and installations detailed here, the human is still positioned at the centre of the universe – or the top of the food chain. The visuals are arranged according to our sensory preferences. They are designed by us, for us. To go beyond this, we would need to decentre our own species and position ourselves as being truly collaborative and cooperative within interspecies relationships. A truly more-than-human future might not always be convenient, or preferable, for the human.

The Earth Species Project aims to use AI to understand more-than-human communication, building on advances in machine learning that have made it possible to translate human languages from scratch. The project could ultimately advance non-human forms of nature from bearing witness to human decisions made on their behalf to making their own decisions. This development would open up myriad ethical and philosophical questions. Kay Firth-Butterfield, who serves on the board of the project and is Head of AI and Machine Learning at the World Economic Forum, has noted that 'understanding what animals say is the first step to giving other species on the planet "a voice" in conversations on our environment. For example, should whales be asked to dive out of the way of boats when this fundamentally changes their feeding or should boats change course?'[18]

Considering where the responsibility for change or adaptation lies will become increasingly important as human relationships with other parts of nature become more fraught. A recently published review study led by researchers at the University of Washington found that human–wildlife conflicts are rising as humans and animals alike are forced by climate breakdown to seek out new habitats and new water and food sources. The paper examined 49 cases of human–wildlife conflict on land and at sea, finding that 43% of studies reported injury to people and 45% reported injury to animals.[19]

DESIGNING SYMBIOSIS

If we decentre humans, what kinds of environments and experiences will emerge? Artist Alexandra Daisy Ginsberg's Pollinator Pathmaker provides a powerful early answer to this question. Launched in 2021, the algorithmic design tool aims to change our perspective on the audience of a garden. Created for animals and cared for by humans, the tool makes plans for gardens that are planted according to the needs and cycles of pollinators (bees, butterflies, wasps, beetles and more) that emerge in particular seasons, sense the world radically differently to us and have distinct foraging patterns. The algorithm optimises its output to cater to the most diverse array of pollinators possible, a decision that was made on the basis of maximising empathy. Once a digital garden has been created, you can fly through it and apply pollinator vision to experience an approximation of how its users would see it.

In a more-than-human future, buildings and structures will be designed to attract and nurture multispecies life, rather than repelling or minimising it. ECOncrete makes sea walls with shapes and textures designed to be appealing to sea organisms. As more organisms make a home on the concrete, the wall is enhanced by their presence. Scientist and ECOncrete co-founder Shimrit Perkol-Finkel explains: 'As time goes by, more marine invertebrates attach to the surface and grow into oysters, corals, and other calcitic structures. The organisms add weight and a layer of bioprotection that makes the concrete armouring more effective, and longer lasting.'[20]

Reggio School, an experimental school in suburban Madrid designed by architects Office for Political

Innovation, features a range of more-than-human design elements, including recessed gardens that are inaccessible to humans but open and welcoming to butterflies, birds and bees. The building has been sprayed with a cork mixture that will attract insects and fungi over its lifetime, with the aim of it becoming as full of life as a tree.

(Artist Magdalena Abakanowicz's Arboreal Architecture, proposed for Paris in the 1990s, seems prescient here, with its underground roots and stretching branches. The artist saw all of life as being made up of fibres – from leaves to muscles and veins.[21])

A more-than-human mindset entails thinking not in terms of hierarchies, or even partnerships, but in terms of relationships. In the article 'Calling for a More-Than-Human Politics', designer and futurist Anab Jain assembles a field guide for the practice of a more-than-human politics and writes that 'we need to reject the division within ourselves, between ourselves, and from the deep ecology that sustains us'.[22] Relational design strategist Sabrina Meherally is the founder of Pause and Effect, a decolonial design and research think tank and consultancy that uses a framework of relational design to 'challenge the colonial limitations of Human Centred Design, and... shift towards practices which cultivate responsibility for our collective and individual impact on people, land, and systems'.[23]

Living in more-than-human symbiosis means bringing the natural world into your sphere of care, and interacting with it for reasons that extend beyond human benefit. Designer Ance Janevica's pollination equipment invites humans to take up pollination as a leisure activity to ensure that the vital process occurs even as populations of insects and other pollinators are depleted. A suit, footwear, UV goggles and jewellery-like finger extensions enable wearers to locate appropriate plants and receive their pollen for distribution.

In 2020, the touring exhibition *Plant Fever* published a Manifesto of Phyto-centred Design. Its seven proposed actions include 'boycott monoculture', 'design with plants' and 'restore the ancient alliance: seek partnerships based on reciprocity'.

Designing for the benefit of multiple species will also mean learning from other species. Biologist Janine Benyus popularised the idea of biomimicry – creating designs and innovations that emulate nature's processes. 'The best way to design for life is to learn from life,' she told the Royal Society of Arts in 2022, 'and that's the essence of biomimicry. Valuing nature not for what we can extract, harvest or domesticate, but for what we can learn.'[24] Biomimicry 3.8, her consultancy, works with companies to teach them to design with nature and learn from it. It created the website AskNature.org to be a repository of design solutions drawn from nature, organised by sector for designers and engineers to browse.

Writer and artist James Bridle is working with researchers in Greece to create Server Farm, a project that will make a computer in collaboration with plants and other lifeforms. Its first output, Test Plot 001, involves growing the materials for the computer using three types of hyperaccumulators: plants that grow in metal-rich soils and accumulate metals such as nickel, zinc and cadmium in their leaves and stems, leaving the soil remediated and ready for use by other plants or animals. Bridle suggests that, in the future, we could use these cultivation techniques instead of relying on the extractive, destructive and polluting technique of mining.

Products designed from a more-than-human mindset will be designed to be nature-positive, or regenerative, in their production. Buyers of truly regenerative products will need to accept that they are purchasing a very different type of item: one that changes, is not homogeneous, and will hopefully – if it succeeds in its purpose – one day become permanently unavailable. This type of product design will require a different way of thinking and planning: the business model behind it is sometimes described as 'start up, shut down'.

Alga Vodka, a concept developed by designer Kit Ondaatje Rolls with the regenerative luxury platform

Maison/o, is an early example, and shows the potential of luxury products to dominate this sector. The vodka is made by harvesting harmful, human-made algal blooms, which have a high fermentable sugar content. In keeping with the root-to-stem approach found in nature, where nothing is wasted, the algal biomass is also used as pigments and cardboard for the product's packaging.

Designer Sebastian Cox's furniture company makes products with a nature-first perspective. Wood is coppiced from local managed woodlands, where young trees are harvested a decade after planting to allow in light and increase biodiversity in the area. The first aim of the woodland management plan is to boost biodiversity; the second is to yield wood. If the wood was not cut, it argues in the company's environmental policy, the benefits to biodiversity would not occur. 'We're actually accidentally mimicking with our chainsaws the activity of woolly mammoths and giant herbivores that used to move around our landscape,' Cox told design website *Dezeen* in an interview in 2020.[25]

Further examples of pairings that have interspecies benefits are emerging. In Scotland, the Dornoch Environmental Enhancement Project at Dornoch Firth uses oysters to filter the water used to make whisky. By reintroducing 4 million native oysters to the area by 2030, the project is expected to increase biodiversity by 50% and treble carbon sequestration in the seabed, bringing multiple benefits to multiple species.

By this point, it has probably become clear that humans collaborating on reciprocal terms with other parts of nature can produce powerful results. Let's throw a curveball into the mix here. As more-than-human thinking has grown in influence, it has intersected with the rise of generative AI across technology and wider culture. Tech companies are now edging towards the prospect of developing AGI – artificial general intelligence – which, if it is achieved, will have its own type of sentience. Machine intelligence brings another complex facet to the debate around more-than-human rights and ethics, and this is starting to be examined. The working group Indigenous AI is developing new conceptual approaches to building AI, asking questions such as 'How can Indigenous epistemologies and ontologies contribute to the global conversation regarding society and AI?' and 'How do we imagine a future with AI that contributes to the flourishing of all humans and non-humans?'[26]

The method of using human-and-machine teams to co-create has become known in AI research as a centaur system. Some commentators propose that centaur systems that use a triptych of human, more-than-human, and machine intelligences would be a radically collaborative path to pursue. One AI start-up, Sakana, is drawing inspiration from the collective movements of fish and the ways in which bees coordinate in hives, to create an AI based on collective animal intelligence rather than human brains.

Nature and technology have long been entwined. Even before the current wave of AI provoked more urgent questions around intelligence, theorists were considering the other intelligences and capabilities that machines exhibited. In a 1987 article published in *Whole Earth Review*, biologist Lynn Margulis and ecological theorist Dorion Sagan compared machines to viruses and beehives, stating that they are able to reproduce and evolve.[27] In a more-than-human future, they may evolve alongside, and even as part of, nature.

REWILDING WORLDS

In the face of drastic biodiversity loss, habitat and animal restoration are increasingly being viewed as priorities worldwide. Successful rewilding demands empathy as well as careful preparation and ongoing observation and adjustment, as it must meet the needs of multiple species, not only human preferences. This means, for example, thinking beyond parks – invented by humans to sanitise nature, arranging it neatly for our consumption – to more truly wild spaces, in which nature takes charge again.

There have been many examples of successful rewilding programmes around the world in recent years. The UK has reintroduced wild bison, beavers, ponies and pigs; the Netherlands is home to wild horses, deer and wolves; lynx have been reintroduced across France, Germany and Switzerland. 'Sea wilding' has restored oyster beds and seagrass; 'rewetting' has restored peatlands and marshlands. South China tigers, previously limited to zoos, have been rewilded in South Africa, demonstrating that rewilding does not always mean the exact recreation of past circumstances. (Writer Warren Ellis has called rewilding 'future-wilding', precisely because 'conditions of eight thousand years ago can only be approximated', and it is wiser to think in terms of 'not what it was, but what it could become'.[28])

The timescales involved in rewilding extend far into the past, but also long into the future. Long-term thinking is core: planning for woodland management extends to a 200-year timeline in some cases.

Public support for rewilding projects is strong – a 2021 YouGov poll commissioned by the charity Rewilding Britain found that 81% of British people support rewilding, with only 5% opposed[29] – and funding is growing: the organisation Rewilding Europe has been awarded over £4 million to expand its rewilding landscapes to around 8 million hectares by 2030. The word itself is divisive among farmers and landowners, as it could potentially both harm their livelihoods and move land use away from agriculture. (Some practitioners refer to 'restoration' rather than rewilding for this reason.) A counterargument is that rewilding opens up opportunities for ecotourism – as it has at Knepp, a former wheat farm and rewilding success story in the UK – and, when led by local communities, can create new jobs.

It could also have major positive effects on humans' mental health. A 2019 study by a team led by Dr Mathew White at the University of Exeter Medical School found that areas richer in biodiversity brought about higher levels of stress reduction in people who spent time in them.[30] Miles Richardson, Professor of Human Factors and Nature Connectedness at the University of Derby, is researching how increased biodiversity in a treescape may increase the wellbeing of humans – for example, whether more birdsong has a more positive effect.[31]

Rewilding will force the human relationship with wildlife to adapt. Spaces solely for animals will proliferate: humans have started to create wildlife corridors that protect animals on their migratory routes. They will also act as 'climate corridors' as the earth heats and animals need to disperse and migrate as a result. Future maps of national travel networks – rivers, roads, walking routes – could also feature more-than-human wayfinding. Seeing this wayfinding in action will be a startling experience to people who have grown used to depleted animal populations: if they return, we'll again get used to skies that are noticeably darkened by flocks of birds overhead, cacophonous with communication.

Shared space will need to be negotiated. This will sometimes happen at an individual level, much like we share borders and boundaries with neighbours at present. In Wales, a household recently discovered a wild beaver – unheard of for the area – felling trees in their garden. Despite the surprise destruction, they currently live happily alongside it, and have expressed a desire for the beaver to stay and thrive in its new home. Equally positive effects on human–animal interaction have been observed on a larger scale in Wellington, New Zealand. The 225-hectare ecosanctuary Zealandia opened 20 years ago in the city, with the aim of restoring its land to the level of biodiversity it had 700 years prior, before humans, rats and stoats disturbed the ecosystem. The sanctuary's success – sightings of the endangered kākā parrot have more than tripled in the city since 2011, sightings of kererū and tūi birds have more than doubled, and orcas now visit the harbour several times a year – has given Wellington residents greater personal experience of interacting with once-rare animals and mobilised them to begin their own conservation efforts.

However, factoring plants and animals into human-made environments is not always done well and can end up being seen as greenwashing – sustainable-seeming gestures that have little or no impact. Verdant, plant-filled architectural designs are one example of this. Buildings such as 1000 Trees in Shanghai, where 1,000 trees and 250,000 plants sit in concrete planters atop a shopping centre, have been criticised for not being planned with the needs of the vegetation in mind, as well as for releasing more carbon into the atmosphere during the build than the plants will ever reabsorb.[32]

Smaller-scale interventions have also been critiqued. Bee bricks, which can be integrated into conventional brickwork to provide space for solitary bees to nest, have had mixed reviews in terms of efficacy. They can attract mites, may lack the depth that bees require, and may be less effective to bees' overall prosperity than simply planting more nectar-rich flowers. Meanwhile, badly designed insect nesting sites such as insect hotels can lead to parasitism, which kills bees, or mould growth, which leads to disease. Good practice involves careful positioning and yearly maintenance – again underlining the need to think in terms of ongoing relationships.

Spatial design will need to take into account the sensory preferences of more-than-human species, as well as their habitation needs. Human-centred environments are overlit and often filled with sound pollution; a more-than-human landscape will be quieter and darker than we have become accustomed to, feature a radically different colour palette, and possibly have a lot more smells. Most radically, it will be less neat and less controlled. Successful river restoration techniques include 'rewiggling' – placing the bends back into a river – which quickly restores the diversity of life it supports, for example by creating still pools in which fish can lay eggs. If we rewiggle our wider world, will we be comfortable with the results?

The environmental and spatial equity of people as well as other lifeforms will need to be a focus as people redesign their relationships with other parts of nature. Carolyn Finney's 2014 book, *Black Faces, White Spaces: Reimagining the Relationship of African Americans to the Great Outdoors*, explores how nature and access to outdoor spaces are racialised in America, and how white supremacy has shaped perceptions of natural space. The Wilderness Society's Public Lands Curriculum, launched in 2022, covers the history of public land in the US, including atrocities committed against Indigenous people and the racial discrimination and segregation that has taken place on public land.

Rewilding efforts will need to take into account the full history of spaces and places, including the humans who have previously inhabited and tended to them, as well as non-human lifeforms.

Shakara Tyler is a founding member of the US Black food sovereignty group Black Dirt Farm Collective, which is cultivating a decolonial agrarian movement called Afroecology. 'We (re)build topsoil and save seeds not only for biodiversity and eco-regeneration, but for the growth of our souls,' writes Tyler. 'It is a homegoing and homecoming, simultaneously.'[33] Black people lost about 5 million hectares of land in the US over the 20th century and, as of 2016, owned less than 1% of the country's rural land. Black Dirt Farm Collective is made up of returning-generation farmers and has purchased 8 hectares of rural land in Maryland to use as a farm and educational space. It also operates urban farms and community gardens across the US Mid-Atlantic, South Atlantic and Deep South.

Restoration of land rights and community ownership are rising topics of discussion around the world. Satellite imagery published in 2023 by NASA's Earth Observatory shows the recovery that Nepal's diminished forests have made since being placed in the care of local communities. Around 22,000 local groups, or 3 million households, manage 2.3 million hectares in the country. Between 1992 and 2016, forest cover almost doubled, due largely to natural regeneration.

Group buyouts of land are a grassroots way for local collectives to reclaim areas. In Otley, West Yorkshire, in the UK, the group Otley 2030 has successfully purchased the 20-acre East Wood via a crowdfunding campaign, and now plans to steward the wood long-term.

In the US, conservation groups are buying back golf courses to rewild the land.

More nomadic ways of cultivating relationships with nature are also emerging. Black-founded collective Flock Together began in 2020 as a birdwatching club, with chapters in different cities around the world, and has since expanded into a platform that it describes as '[facilitating] many people's first steps into nature, challenging perceptions on what "nature" is and who it belongs to'.[34]

GARDENING YOUR WORLD VIEW

A more-than-human future would require such a fundamental shift in mindset, on such a mass scale, that it may feel impossible to bring this idea into everyday lives in a meaningful way. This is a recurring theme within futures thinking: what is the point in putting the effort into a small-scale individual response if other people, or other companies, or other nations, are not doing the same? Will it make any difference? Particularly within ecologically driven futures visions, the need to push for systemic change is often pitted against taking individual action, as though we can only choose one approach. It's important for change-makers to bear in mind that individual changes can become larger-scale changes, both by creating 'contagion' by inspiring others to act, and also by inspiring bigger changes among the individuals who start small.

Research on social norms places the social tipping point for mainstream adoption of new ideas at roughly 25% of a population. Futures happen slowly, sometimes imperceptibly, and then all at once: as soon as an idea goes mainstream, it can snowball. Change can happen from many directions. It's not only the case that government initiatives influence society and culture and then influence individuals. Change can also – and must also – happen the other way round, and it frequently does.

It can start with a garden. As the only green space that many people have direct control over, the garden is a test bed for biodiversity gains. Campaigns such as No Mow May and 'leave the leaves' are encouraging people to tend their lawns less, take a month off or even reduce mowing to once or twice a year. Proponents of this approach report that insects quickly come back, particularly winged insects, while 'pest' species see no benefit from the change and may even decrease.

Increasing interest in self-sufficiency is seeing people also turn lawn space into more productive projects. US permaculture and community gardening movement Food Not Lawns encourages people to cultivate their gardens into biodiverse ecological homesteads. Larger-scale food forests – also known as forest gardens or living pantries – are being planted in public green spaces to encourage a complete natural ecosystem, and to provide shade and food for neighbourhoods. These are particularly relevant in heat-vulnerable urban areas as temperatures rise and both floods and droughts increase.

As more people focus on rewilding and restoration, seed keeping will become a central purpose for informal groups and DIY networks, as well as for public and private institutions. Community centres increasingly offer seed libraries: the Mystic & Noank public library in Connecticut, USA, offers more than 90 types of seeds, organised in a card catalogue, for anyone with a library card to take home and plant.

At Annapurna, an Indigenous seed library in North-East India, rice farmer Mahan Borah stores and plants more than 400 seed varieties. Other seed savers nurture heirloom seed gardens, growing deep purple corn, kaleidoscope kale and more polyculture wonders that help to preserve global plant diversity.

Anthropologist Dr Natasha Myers speaks of the Planthroposcene, a 'scene in which we seed solidarities with the plants'. She sees this revolution happening in gardens and in kitchens, replacing home economics with 'home ecologics'. 'Planthroposcenes,' Dr Myers told the Society for Cultural Anthropology in 2020, 'can take root in our upturned and liberated lawns, in gardens, on a windowsill, or in a bucket on a stoop with some seeds shared among friends.'[35]

The branding of the new plant care range Sowvital shows how attitudes to plants have changed. Resembling beauty products rather than a more conventional garden centre buy, its three products – plant food, spritz and leaf spray – turn houseplant maintenance into an act that feels more like nurturing a close animal companion or human loved one.

From the seeds planted in more biodiverse gardens, food forests and home ecologics, a generation of more nature-first people could grow, nurtured by regenerative learning practices, to know the names of their more-than-human neighbours, as well as how to live reciprocally alongside them.

One final aspect of more-than-human futures that often goes unexamined in discussions – which is a clear tell of how polarising this issue is – is what we should eat. Plant-based diets and lifestyles have risen in prominence roughly in parallel with increased understanding of animal intelligence and consciousness. Studies put vegans at 1–6% of the population, but flexitarians or plant-forward eaters – who don't ascribe to veganism but are trying to eat less meat and be less reliant on animal products, for myriad reasons – are seeing much bigger increases. A 2022 survey of 4,000 people in France, Germany, Italy and Spain found that 57%

had reduced their meat consumption over the past five years.[36] In addition, 33% of Americans are actively trying to eat less meat and poultry.[37]

As more research on plant intelligence is added to our body of knowledge, some commentators are starting to question the ethics of eating plants. Animal rights activist Earthling Ed's thoughtful response to this nascent debate considers the overall impact to life. 'Even if we were to think that plants could feel and suffer,' he said, 'veganism would still be the most ethical lifestyle because it eliminates the biggest driver of animal suffering and death, and also reduces the biggest cause of deforestation, habitat loss and plant deaths.'[38] Natasha Myers, anthropologist and advocate for the Planthroposcene, says: 'Don't worry: reverence for plants doesn't mean you can't eat them. But it does mean it would be polite to thank them for their generosity.'[39]

The pieces of evidence that more-than-human thinking is gaining ground – or to use trend-forecasting language, the bigger drivers and smaller signals that give weight to this thinking – are widespread, but are clustered significantly across scientific, philosophical, creative and technological spheres. The roots of this future vision lie in major shifts in intellectual enquiry and scientific study, and have spread to gain political will and public enthusiasm. More-than-human futures could bring about the environmental empathy that we badly need to experience to regenerate our planet, but beyond that, they could change how we want to live and how we see ourselves – as one species among many.

2

Degrowth

'The obsession with productivity, and the protection of our economy above all else, seems more and more like a sickness.'

Author and poet Rebecca Tamás, writing for *Granta*'s website in 2021[1]

Degrowth is an economic theory that proposes a democratically planned reduction in economic output, resource use and overall consumption in high-income countries, shifting national goals from economic growth to improving human wellbeing within planetary boundaries. The French term 'décroissance' (reduction, decrease or degrowth) began to be used by economists and philosophers in Europe in the 1970s; the 1972 book *The Limits to Growth*, lead-authored by Donella H. Meadows, introduced similar themes. The core idea of finite growth traces back further, including to John Stuart Mill, who wrote in 1848 that 'the increase of wealth is not boundless', and that 'at the end of what they term the progressive state lies the stationary state'.[2] Degrowth as a movement gained traction in the 2000s, and the concept it has expanded into is supported by numerous ecological economists, climate activists and policy researchers today.

As well as being ecologically timely, degrowth as a future is attracting more attention in the 2020s because of significant breakthroughs in renewable energy, growing support for a circular economy, and rising societal interest in both curbing inequality and rethinking how big a role work, productivity and money take up in people's lives. In short: now that the technological solutions needed to mitigate climate change are available, the barriers to change are considered to be political and behavioural. Degrowth addresses both.

In some ways, degrowth is both a logical and an obvious idea. As economic historian Dirk Philipsen has pointed out, 'The vast majority of people would agree we should care about the greatest wellbeing of the greatest number within the biophysical limits of the planet, for the most part.'[3] Social inequalities have become more visible and more extreme: a 2024 report by Oxfam, called Inequality Inc., found that from 2020 to 2024, the five richest men in the world doubled their fortunes, while almost 5 billion people globally became poorer.[4] People are becoming more receptive to the idea that redistribution is necessary: in 2020, the 'eat the rich' meme took off across social media, and extreme wealth is now increasingly being linked to ecocide.

In 2023, a survey of 2,000 members of the public conducted by the German Environment Agency found that 88% of respondents agreed with the statement 'we must find ways of living well regardless of economic growth', 77% agreed that 'there are natural limits to growth and we went beyond them' and 73% agreed that 'we should be ready to reduce our living standards'.[5] Meanwhile, a study by Lily Paulson and Milena Büchs, published in 2022, found that 60.5% of people across 34 European countries are in favour of post-growth values including collectivism, distributed power, a sufficiency economy and social justice.[6]

These studies spanned age groups, and this sentiment is emerging across age groups, but there is an important generational context to take into account. The two younger adult generations living in high-income nations today – categorised by marketers as millennials and Gen Z, and born between 1981 and 2012 – have grown up amid financial recessions (many millennials graduated into one) and the environmental crisis;

many will never reach the wealth milestones that their parents experienced. People who are today aged 45 or below may well be inclined to be much less supportive of protecting assets (property, savings) that they simply don't have – particularly when taxing these assets more strongly would instantly address rising inequality and help to create intergenerational and intragenerational equity. A 2022 poll commissioned by the Institute of Economic Affairs (IEA) and Fraser Institute found that 43% of UK respondents supported socialism as their preferred economic system, rising to 53% among 18–34-year-olds.[7]

Even the very wealthy are in favour of redistribution – to some extent. A 2024 poll of 2,300 people who make up the richest 5% of society, holding investable assets of more than US$1 million, found that 74% support higher taxes on wealth to improve public services.[8]

Political figures still largely prioritise economic growth, but alternative framings are gaining traction. Speaking at the EU's 2023 Beyond Growth conference, an event that was first held in 2018 and remains notable for even existing, European Commission President Ursula von der Leyen stated that 'economic growth is not an end in itself. That growth must not destroy its own foundations. That growth must serve people and future generations.' Philippe Lamberts, the Green MEP who organised the event, told the *Financial Times* that 'discussing these things is no longer seen as sacrilege'.[9] In 2018, national governments formed the Wellbeing Economy Governments partnership – currently comprising six countries – to share policy developments that enable them to develop economies that foreground the wellbeing of people and planet.

Official cross-governmental bodies are increasingly acknowledging degrowth and highlighting the challenges it addresses. In 2022, for the first time since its original report was published in 1990, the Intergovernmental Panel on Climate Change (IPCC) featured degrowth by name in a report on climate impacts, adaptation and vulnerability. Degrowth was identified as a pathway to a sustainable future in a 2022 report by the Intergovernmental Science-Policy Platform on Biodiversity and Ecosystem Services (IPBES), and UN officials have begun to acknowledge overconsumption by rich people in high-income nations as a problem that needs to be addressed to meet environmental goals and limit climate breakdown.

Even as some warm to its ideas, political and corporate figures tend to be very wary of the word 'degrowth', which carries negative connotations of regressing back to past, less prosperous, states of being. 'Growth', as a word, is associated with flourishing, and is seen as natural and largely positive: children grow, plants grow, and when people work hard, their incomes and their businesses grow. There have been many discussions around whether to change the term, which is common within futures thinking. If a concept becomes politicised or divisive or is overtly rejected, when should you stay with it, and when should the language used to describe a possible future be adjusted, abandoned or rebranded? Economic anthropologist and prominent degrowth scholar Jason Hickel has suggested using degrowth as a technical term in academic contexts, where a substantial body of research and writing already exists, while in public contexts emphasising elements such as community decision-making and improving health and wellbeing. 'What matters is that the principles are reflected in policies,' he has said. 'Then you can call it whatever you want.'[10] Jeremy Williams, co-founder of the Post Growth Institute and co-author of *The Economics of Arrival*, told me that 'post-growth, or degrowth, has been defined by what it is against, rather than what it's for', making it inherently limited in appeal. 'What we're really talking about is the wisdom to tell good growth from bad growth, and be able to choose more carefully between them.'

It's important to note too that degrowth should be a process, not an end result; if achieved, degrowth would lead to an economic system based on a steady-state economy. Such an economy would effectively operate within economist Kate Raworth's doughnut economics model, which describes the ring of space that provides people with the social foundations essential for life while stopping short of the earth's ecological ceiling. The sweet spot in the middle – the doughnut – combines ecological security with social justice.

One of the main strengths of the word 'degrowth', however divisive it may be, is that it clearly articulates the problem and faces it head-on. Other approaches to rethinking growth do not, although they might sound easier and more appealing. Green growth presents a more commercially and politically palatable approach, but it doesn't address the core problem of growth: the fundamental mindset it represents that more is always coming, and that more will be inherently better. Other economists advocate for growth-agnostic or post-growth approaches, while in business and politics decoupling has become an overarching aim for sustainability strategy, promising economic growth without environmental impact. Some brands have started to set and achieve goals to decouple their economic growth from their use of resources, often by recycling some materials, or to decouple their economic growth from their emissions by switching to renewable energy and using carbon offsetting. While some of these strategies are innovative and forward-looking, they don't present a scalable, systemic solution, because they don't tackle the central issues of environmental degradation, consumerism and our ever-growing need for more.

Even self-defined critics of degrowth acknowledge that economic growth has slowed in advanced economies and that an alternative framework will be necessary. It is becoming more widely accepted that gross domestic product (GDP) is not an effective metric for measuring national prosperity, and that more expansive measures that take into account all contributions to society, including unpaid work such as care, should be developed.

The other major critique of degrowth is that it focuses on the economic circumstances of the Global North, which is responsible for 74% of global excess material use and 92% of excess CO_2 emissions, while ignoring the needs of people in the Global South, whose countries have historically been extracted from.[11] Some advocates for degrowth link it overtly to decolonial principles, including within its remit the requirement to provide reparations from the Global North to the Global South, cancel debt and facilitate environmental and social justice. Another way of seeing it is that implementing a global economic agenda set by the Global North's actions and needs is still using colonial practices. A paper published in 2019 by authors including Beatriz Rodríguez-Labajos captured the issue succinctly: 'Once again, an idea is launched to the world with an undeniable Eurocentric origin.'[12] This is an inherent tension, and given that degrowth as a movement is so interested in examining and critiquing power structures, it will need to be continually addressed. As philosopher and cultural theorist Kate Soper has said, 'Affluent societies should not be enjoying a monopoly over ideas of progress and the so-called "good life" or allowed to provide the only model of how to develop.'[13] This may be one area where the idea of plural futures becomes very visible and applicable: researchers Corinna Dengler and Lisa Marie Seebacher have written that degrowth can be seen as 'a Northern supplement to Southern concepts, movements and lines of thought' and should seek alliances with social and environmental justice movements in the Global South to align with 'fellow travellers'.[14]

A global project to distribute resources equitably and rethink consumption, production and quality of life probably sounds somewhat daunting. It could also be energising and rewarding, giving us what is for many people a much-needed opportunity to redesign the systems we live within. As Samuel Alexander, academic director of the Simplicity Institute and a long-time advocate for degrowth, has written: 'Human beings find creative projects fulfilling, and the challenge of building the new world within the shell of the old promises to be immensely meaningful, even if it will also entail times of trial.'[15]

DESIGNING TRANSITIONS

Degrowth revolves around acknowledging and accepting that materially we are at the end of more. Transitioning to a degrowth-oriented future will therefore mean working with what we already have. The task is to design transitions: to plant the new system within the soil of the existing system and biodegrade the ideas and practices that are no longer fit for purpose, while creating the space for new ideas and practices to grow. This will need to happen at every level, from grassroots organisations and individual decisions to a whole-government approach of policies, incentives, investment and taxes.

The basic infrastructure that would need to be put into place for degrowth is in some ways already happening, for example, in the shift to renewable energy and increased energy efficiency. In other areas, particularly where the change is social rather than technological, the shift will feel more radical, stretching the Overton window wider.

The foundational elements of putting degrowth in practice include building out a raft of universal basic services provided by state-owned infrastructure and spanning healthcare, education and training, and access to the internet and nutritious food. Campaigners and academics advocate for a Climate Job Guarantee, a government initiative to retrain people in decarbonising roles – showing how degrowth strategies would grow some sectors while phasing out others. A similar idea, though differently contextualised, was put into action by the US government in 2023 with the announcement of the American Climate Corps, a skills-based training programme to equip young people for careers in clean energy. Jobs in maintenance, repair and upkeep are likely to grow: the fastest-growing job over the next decade, according to the US Bureau of Labor Statistics, will be wind turbine technician – a well-paid role that doesn't require a college degree.

Alongside job guarantees, there are increasing numbers of trials piloting universal basic income (UBI) programmes, which can enjoy high public support (around 75% in the UK, according to a study by pressure group Compass[16]). In Kenya, the world's largest and longest UBI scheme, involving almost 5,000 people, began in 2017 and will run to 2029; participants have been observed to seek out fulfilling long-term work, including starting their own businesses, while other trials have linked receiving UBI to increases in wellbeing. Some see UBI as an idea whose time has come, while others view it as permanently politically and economically unviable.

Shorter working weeks are another popular policy idea that could act as a catalyst to degrowth, by spurring people to rethink how they approach productivity and work–life balance and opening up possibilities for different lifestyles and community dynamics to emerge. The idea has gained momentum since the pandemic began, and trials have been conducted around the world. A large-scale study of four-day, 32-hour work week trials across 91 companies in the US, the UK, Ireland and Canada found that there was no overall impact on productivity or intensity of work, that stress and burnout decreased overall, and that participants felt better able to combine paid work with care responsibilities. They were also able to spend slightly more time on hobbies and volunteering.[17] In the UK, the New Economics Foundation has proposed shortening the standard paid work week further, to 21 hours in high-income countries, to address overwork and help to rebalance employment rates.[18] While the idea may not work for every job and every industry, it is fast becoming an expectation for progressive and ethically minded businesses to at least be discussing shortened work weeks and much more flexible working patterns.

Even with work weeks shortened or basic income installed, so long as business models are designed to prioritise growth and maximise shareholder return, degrowth will not be able to succeed. Shareholder primacy is a difficult framework to challenge because it is so dominant within corporate governance, but it is not impossible. Several alternative business models are emerging that counter this mindset and enable companies and organisations to operate with different strategies. To achieve B Corp certification, for example, companies are legally required to change their constitutional documents to stakeholder-focused decision-making. Dutch chocolate maker Tony's Chocolonely has allocated 'golden shares' to its appointed Mission Guardians, a group of people with the power to prevent legal changes to its governance and mission and to speak out publicly or privately if concerns are raised to them by any stakeholder. UK-based business Library of Things uses a similar mechanism to lock in its mission and keep its directors accountable to its values over the long term. The Better Business Act, a campaign supported by more than 2,500 businesses, is working to make this level of responsibility not a choice but a legal requirement in the UK, so that all companies must align social and environmental needs with shareholders' interests, by default.

In the tech industry, it has become highly aspirational for businesses to become unicorns – privately owned start-ups that are valued at US$1 billion or more. An alternative approach sees businesses aiming to be zebras. As defined by the cooperative group Zebras Unite, 'Zebra companies are both black and white: they are profitable and improve society. They won't sacrifice one for the other.'[19] Zebras aim to become financially self-sustaining but seek investors who see impact as part of their return on investment. And where unicorns often aim to disrupt, zebras aim to 'repair, cultivate, and connect'.[20] In 2023, the Japanese government highlighted zebra companies in its economic plans as a key model for enhancing the vitality of small and medium-sized businesses, marking the first policy development to be driven by the movement.

Constructing the new system within the shell of the old is essential to degrowth in a figurative sense, but applies more literally, too. Existing physical infrastructure will be repurposed to meet new and growing needs: in Scotland, decommissioned on-street broadband cabinets are being repurposed into charging points for electric vehicles (EVs); in Paris, a former steam railway ring has been converted into green space, a natural cooling solution to help the city prepare for the effects of extreme heat. Manufacturers are transitioning too: as sales of heat pumps outpace sales of gas furnaces, businesses are switching from making gas boilers to producing their replacements. In architecture, retrofit-first policies seek to make sensitive use of what is already in place – in the UK, 80% of the buildings we have today will still exist in 2050, and of the estimated 39% of energy-related CO_2 emissions that buildings contribute globally each year, 11% comes from materials and construction.[21]

These decisions are pragmatic, and driven by necessity, but there is a beauty to living within the history and remnants of past ideas, technologies and lifestyles. People are fascinated by ruins, relics and artefacts, and the aesthetic of degrowth – keeping visible the layers of how we lived before, and how we chose to change – could be deeply poetic. UK-based recycled plastics company Smile Plastics produces recycled surfaces made from materials including plastic packaging, CDs, medical equipment and electric cables. One surface is made from tinsel, a material that used to be highly positive, symbolising celebration and festivity, but is now also negative, symbolising microplastic pollution and material wastefulness. By rehabbing the tinsel into beautiful worktop surfaces, it's made useful and positive once again.

The role of the designer is changing from always creating the new to focusing first on redesigning, subtracting where necessary, and considering repair and reuse as essential parts of the user experience. In South Korea, design studio one-aftr used an adaptive reuse approach to refit three disused industrial buildings, which had become overgrown with plants, into a cafe that treats the plants as an interior garden, with intact sections gently refitted for humans to occupy safely. In this way, the space retains its history and tells a story that a new build would have bulldozed.

Rotterdam-based architecture practice Studio Ossidiana describes maintenance as 'a slow design act'.[22] It can also be very joyful: designer Phoebe Flatau envisages a new nocturnal workforce, called the disassemblers, who approach maintenance and community care as a form of carnival. In Flatau's vision, the workforce dismantles structures that are at the end of their life through the night, salvaging materials for reuse.

During the degrowth process of physical and social transition, we'll be scaffolding our world view – methodically and consistently – to change what we consider to be 'more' and 'better'. In many ways, this means shifting from 'more for the few' to 'better for the vast majority', including both people living today and future generations.

LESS MEANING MORE

Strikingly similar ideas about the need to degrow lifestyles are starting to emerge organically across societies. In Japan, the book *Capital in the Anthropocene*, published in 2020, has been a surprise smash hit, selling 500,000 copies by 2022. Written by philosopher Kohei Saito, it advocates for the principles and process of post-capitalism degrowth in line with the writings of Karl Marx, and was published in English with the title *Marx in the Anthropocene: Towards the Idea of Degrowth*

Communism. Prior to its publication, the seeds were already sown for a changing mindset: Japan experienced low consumer confidence in the 2010s, creating what management consultant Kenichi Ohmae termed a 'low-desire society', with young people saving rather than spending. In China, the *tang ping* (lying flat) movement took off in 2021, with young people protesting against a culture of overwork by choosing to relax and work less. In the US, the quiet quitting trend has more recently advocated for similar acts of resistance, while in Europe, the term 'limitarianism' – coined by Belgian philosopher Ingrid Robeyns, who proposes adding an upper limit to income and wealth – has gained some traction.

The lockdowns of the early pandemic in 2020 oxygenated these nascent impulses, with many people sitting at home scrutinising the news, their lives and all the stuff they owned in more detail than perhaps they had before.

Globally, we continue to move in the wrong direction with our use of raw materials and energy and overall consumption. The 2024 Circularity Gap Report found that over the five years from 2018 to 2023, people used 500 gigatonnes of resources, which is 28% of all the materials humanity has consumed since 1900.[23] In that same time period, consumption rose and circularity declined. The UN reports that, at current rates, extraction of raw materials is set to rise 60% by 2060.[24]

In the book *Thinking in Systems*, first written in 1993 and published in 2008, Donella H. Meadows articulated the situation we find ourselves in. 'For any physical entity in a finite environment, perpetual growth is impossible. Ultimately, the choice is not to grow forever, but to decide what limits to live within.'[25] Increasingly, people are sensing the need for these limits, and imposing them on themselves.

Canada-based illustrator Sarah Lazarovic spent a year dealing with the urge to impulse-buy items by painting them instead. The result was the book *A Bunch of Pretty Things I Did Not Buy*, which captures one of the challenges of degrowth lifestyles — how do we self-actualise if we cannot shop? — by channelling the thrill of consumerism into a creative outlet. Other creatives have adapted to find pleasure in the act of frugality itself. The Buy Nothing movement organises sharing communities worldwide, with 10 million people giving and receiving 2.6 million items each month; on Chinese social network Douban, a number of self-organised online groups around degrowth lifestyles have formed, including Minimalist Life, Consumption Culture Betrayers, Low Consumption Research Institute, and If We Could Be Happy Without Consumption.

In 2022, the Hot or Cool Institute released a report on 'resizing fashion for a fair consumption space', finding that an 80% reduction in clothes shopping would be needed for the richest inhabitants of high-income countries, including the UK, Italy and Germany, to achieve a sufficiency scenario of fair consumption.[26] This was distilled into the 'rule of five', a limit of five new fashion purchases a year, which fashion industry professionals including writer Tiffanie Darke and retail consultant Jane Shepherdson have since taken up as a challenge. Documenting the experience, they have recounted finding that the constraint has made them enjoy the creativity of dressing more, rather than less, by encouraging them to re-wear, re-tailor and customise their existing clothes. Businesses are similarly finding ways to redirect the thrill of buying new by making the experience of getting an item repaired or re-tailored feel both easier and more luxurious, so that it delivers some of those same feelings of pleasure and excitement.

Trends in aesthetic self-expression will still exist, and are likely to become more diverse and more creative, but buying less, using items for longer and caring for them to prolong their lifespan is the most immediate way for people to tackle overproduction and overconsumption. Across the consumer product sector, items have become disposable in how we treat them but almost permanent in how long they live in landfill, due to being made largely of plastic.

Innovative retailers and urban planners are using recycling to transition the social ritual of physical shopping into a degrowth-led experience. In Eskilstuna in Sweden, a recycling shopping centre made up of 14 shops selling only used and recycled goods is positioned next to the city's resource collection centre, enabling people to responsibly dispose of used goods and acquire necessary replacements in the same leisure outing. In Berlin, the Re-Use superstore is a city-run recycling department store; the city plans to open three or four of these, estimating that every household in the city contains around 244 items that are functional but unused.

While this mindset is growing organically, incentivised reductions of use and consumption will be needed to mainstream a culture of sufficiency within the time span needed. These could include mechanisms such as landfill taxes and carbon taxes for businesses and for individuals, as well as true price and extended producer responsibility laws that require companies to pay in full for the materials, labour and supply chains they use, and take end-of-life responsibility for the products they sell and the waste they generate. These mechanisms could be linked to a public income, whereby the revenue generated is returned to the public, either in visibly environmentally beneficial ways or as a cash dividend.

In the UK, the water regulator Ofwat has considered discounting the water bills of people who install water butts and keep their front gardens planted and unpaved, and is trialling dynamic charging that rewards people who reduce their water use. Around 45 countries now operate deposit return schemes that add an additional charge to drinks, which is then returned to the customer when they return the plastic, glass or metal packaging for reuse or recycling. Adopted in 2019, France's circular economy law requires shops to accept refillable containers and reward customers who use refillable cups with lower-priced drinks, while public-access buildings must offer drinking fountains. These habits quickly become normalised, and while single-use packaging feels convenient, many people have come to realise that its convenience masks untenable levels of waste and pollution. A 2022 survey by market research company Ipsos for Plastic Free July found that 75% of people across 28 countries agree that single-use plastics should be banned as soon as possible.[27]

Many of these mechanisms used to be in place across society in various ways, and for some people their reintroduction could feel like a return to frugality rather than progress. Notably, these schemes can be effective today because of modern technology, which allows items to be scanned, identified and tracked, and the data aggregated and published to keep people accountable. Artificial intelligence could have a very positive impact here, as computer vision can be used to identify and sort items quickly and accurately, significantly improving recycling rates. In this way, and perhaps unexpectedly, degrowth can be high-tech and cutting-edge, supporting and rewarding innovation.

Much of the power of degrowth as a mainstream future will come from changing how we meet our needs, from often individual choices, such as shopping and consuming, to practices and lifestyles that are based around shared value and attaching meaning, reward and self-worth to those acts.

LOCALISM AND COMMUNALISM

If we're buying less, we'll probably be making more, sharing more or renting more. Either way, we will be getting more hands-on with the services and infrastructure in our local communities, creating public wealth rather than private wealth. A future of decreased consumption will create room for spaces that are not shops and increase demand for leisure activities that are not shopping. This could enable spaces like arts centres, youth centres and libraries to reclaim their roles as community hubs, joined by skill-sharing destinations such as maker-spaces and repair cafes.

Degrowth has attracted political interest, but it is not a bipartisan concept, and like other futures before it, it has become politicised. With a number of the world's governments shifting to the right, its proof-of-concepts will come initially from community-scale organisations that are implementing similar ideas. These organisations are using 'everyday politics', defined by civic futures organisation Dark Matter Labs as 'community centred activities that reconnect citizens with public life'.[28]

These initiatives are decentralised and heterogeneous: they will look different in different places and play out in numerous ways across communities and countries, because they will be working with the materials, resources and contexts unique to them. But they share some commonalities and often have a spirit of connected localism, distributing best-practice learnings and processes to be adapted by others to their own scale and needs.

'City portraits' and 'neighbourhood doughnuts' translate the principles of economist Kate Raworth's doughnut economics to cities and communities, creating regenerative economies that are distributive by design. One of the most prominent of these numerous ongoing projects is Amsterdam, which aims to reduce its use of primary raw materials by 50% by 2030 and be 100% circular by 2050. This includes shortening its food supply chains to create a strong regional food system.

Started in 2005 in Totnes in the UK, the Transition movement has now spread to over 48 countries and uses participatory methods to bring about low-carbon, socially just communities and projects. Outcomes are wide-ranging, from repair cafes in Pasadena to rainwater harvesting in São Paulo and community gardens in France.

Other communities are on self-guided and no less ambitious transitions. The Galápagos Islands aims to achieve a net zero carbon footprint by 2040, including a shift to renewable energy via a local wind farm and solar-powered water heaters and the installation of 42 kilometres of cycle paths. Its 2030 strategy includes the goal of adopting the responsible use and consumption of resources as a cultural value.

This move towards localisation and cultural responsibility extends to everything we make, do and organise – even theatre. One of the most innovative examples of decreased consumption in action is director Katie Mitchell's production of *A Play for the Living in a Time of Extinction*. This is a touring play that travels without actors or materials; instead, it is staged by local creatives and performed by a different cast in each venue. A touring score provides the guidelines for staging it, including that the set and costumes should be produced locally and ideally sourced second-hand. By removing travel and a considerable amount of waste, it has minimised its environmental impact while touring Europe and has been performed in Taipei.

Studies indicate that when people have personally participated in a project, they attach greater meaning and value to its outcome. A 2011 study in which people were asked to assemble IKEA furniture found that they were willing to pay 63% more for furniture they had assembled themselves – but that the increased value only applied to projects they had successfully completed.[29]

In the context of the commons, a similar psychology holds true. As more people participate and see the positive impact of their efforts, a snowball effect is created: they want to participate more themselves, and they want to bring their friends in. Conversely, seeing others not participating – and not contributing to the greater good – has a demotivating effect on those who have put work and effort in. The solution is to keep creating momentum, however small, and to show how progress is growing. This can mean micro acts of neighbourliness: Texas-based nonprofit The Better Block developed front-garden retrofit kits to show people how to construct simple flat-pack book-swap tables and conviviality benches for their porches. It can also mean stretching those acts to a global scale: the app Clean Something For Nothing brings together local litter pickers to organise clean-ups and shows the results on maps that zoom out from local to planetary.

One of the largest scales for this principle to be applied is participative democracy. Shared, participatory decision-making processes such as citizens' assemblies put crucial national decisions in the hands of ordinary people, and largely find that they do the research, consider the facts, find common ground and make good decisions. Participants are selected by lottery, in a process similar to jury duty, and their responsibility and access to power don't extend long-term, with the responsibilities of governance spread across many shoulders.

Community-run decision-making took on new importance during the cost-of-living crisis, which began in 2021. As inflation and rising interest rates changed people's spending patterns and caused some businesses to struggle and others to fail, community-owned organisations showed higher-than-average resilience. In the UK, the democratic economy was worth £87.9 billion as of 2023, according to data from Co-operatives UK, with the numbers of community-owned pubs up by 62% in the past five years and employee-owned businesses up by 37% in 12 months.[30]

Community-owned and community-operated neighbourhoods are likely to emerge more formally in the future as people coalesce around shared values, and some early examples are already starting to show the possibilities of how these could look and work. Culdesac Tempe, in Arizona, is the first car-free neighbourhood to be built from scratch in the US. Designed to be walkable and offering a free metro system and lots of bike parking, its private rental apartments are arranged around shared outdoor spaces, which include fire pits, grills and hammocks. In Melbourne, Urban Coup is a 29-household co-housing building, where each household has its own apartment, including a kitchen and bathroom, but shares communal spaces such as a kitchen and dining area, laundry, guest rooms, outdoor space and workshop. Resources and tasks – including childcare – can be more easily shared, and items bought in bulk and then distributed. There are 36 co-housing projects registered across Australia, and interest is growing in the possibility of establishing more.

The Harvard Study of Adult Development, a longitudinal study that tracked three generations of more than 2,000 people over 85 years, found that social connections correlated highly with quality of life. 'The people who were happiest, who stayed healthiest as they grew old, and who lived the longest were the people who had the warmest connections with other people,' said the study's director, Robert Waldinger.[31]

Systems designers have similar insights. As environmentalist Paul Hawken has said, 'You heal a system, whether it is an ecosystem, social system or an immune system, by (re)connecting more of it to itself.'[32] This is also true of transport systems, which include two sectors that make large contributions to greenhouse gas emissions and will need to play a central role in a degrowth-focused future.

LOW-CARBON TRANSPORT

The travel and transport industries have invested a lot of time and money in making themselves desirable and indispensable to our ideas of freedom, growth and success. We self-actualise through travel and prize the convenience and independence associated with owning a car. And increasingly, the true status symbol of extreme wealth is not only taking frequent holidays to far-flung places, but owning a private jet to get you there.

The size of the global private jet fleet more than doubled between 2000 and 2022.[33] These flights are more than 10 times as polluting per passenger as commercial flights, and their emissions have increased by 23% in the few years since the pandemic began. Airports are starting to put measures in place to address the outsize impact of private jets on both carbon emissions and noise pollution: Amsterdam's Schiphol is gradually tightening its rules, decreasing its capacity for private jets in 2024 and aiming to ban them by 2026. This is not without opposition from airlines and other governments, who have declared the plan controversial.

Calls to ban private jets, or at the very least to more heavily tax and de-incentivise their use, are increasing. More contentiously, we are also beginning to see commercial leisure flights as an unsustainable indulgence that we simply cannot afford any more. At the same time, they are as popular as ever. The number of flights taken globally has increased steadily over the past two decades, and while the pandemic caused a blip, the industry was recovering by 2023 and is expected to transport 9.4 billion passengers in 2024.[34] As of 2016, the emissions produced by private jets were 4% of total emissions from aviation,[35] and even accounting for the significant rise in their use since then, emissions are still dominated by commercial flying.

One of the ideas that scares people most about the years ahead is that they might have to travel less – no more cheap flights. And while outright bans on plane travel are unlikely to reach mainstream support in the near future, quotas and frequent-flyer taxes could be more feasible, as they would affect a minority of people. In plane travel, like in so many other areas, use is wildly unequal. In America, 12% of people take more than six round trips by air each year, representing two-thirds of the country's flights, according to research from the International Council on Clean Transportation.[36] In the UK, 70% of flights are made by 15% of people,[37] and citizens' assemblies have supported the idea of taxing people who fly more.

A similar situation has developed in car use, where bigger and more polluting vehicles have become a status symbol. Developed initially as military vehicles and then proving useful for farmers and rural communities, SUVs have dominated new car sales in the US for years and now lead car sales worldwide, making up 51% of sales.[38] Cars sold in Europe have become wider every year since 2001, and this car bloat or 'autobesity' now means that half of new cars cannot fit in parking spaces. Because they are heavier and taller, bigger cars are more lethal in crashes, cut off the visibility of children and cyclists, and are more polluting. Climate activist group Tyre Extinguishers targets SUVs used in urban areas for this reason, deflating their tyres and leaving an explanatory leaflet on the car for its owner to read.

Cities are under pressure to take action to right-size their transport, in part by making it less convenient to drive large cars. In 2024, Paris voted to triple the price of on-street parking for bigger cars, including SUVs. The organisation Adfree Cities has been working to remove the prestige associated with high-emissions products, such as flights and SUVs, by building the case to ban ads of such products. In 2023, they successfully petitioned to have an advert for a Toyota SUV banned, with the UK's Advertising Standards Authority judging that the ad 'had not been prepared with a sense of responsibility to society'.

Much smaller vehicle formats such as micro cars and 'bubble' cars, including the Swiss-made Microlino, are gaining attention and are already popular in some regions: in China, the second most popular electric vehicle (EV) sold in 2022 was a microcar. But a car is still a car: even an EV uses a considerable amount of resources in its manufacture, including rare minerals, the mining of which is environmentally degrading and linked to human rights violations; and like other cars, EVs release polluting microplastics as their tyres wear. Adaptive reuse in the context of road transport could mean expanding public mobility infrastructure and making wiser use of what we already have, such as more buses to make use of the many roads that are already paved. With fewer cars on roads, imaginative new uses for parking spaces will emerge as they become available for other purposes, such as mini green spaces (also known as parklets) or simply wider and more accessible pavements. Initiatives such as Future Station Project are already beginning to speculate on what petrol stations could be turned into when their original use becomes obsolete: suggestions include bike share stations and climate resilience hubs that provide support to people in extreme weather events.

Alternative options for people choosing to be flight-free and car-free are springing up as this market grows, including books that plot out flight-free holiday routes and plans, and specialist travel agents who will organise multi-stop overland holidays for customers, including travel and accommodation, and are contactable via WhatsApp throughout the trip for peace of mind. Employee benefit scheme Climate Perks gives workers paid journey days to incentivise them to switch to flight-free holiday travel, and could become an essential amenity for climate-conscious employees.

Inspiring ideas are emerging that offer preferable alternatives to flying and driving, by re-instilling the pleasure of the journey and the joy of travel in itself as a slower and more enjoyable experience. These include affordable, comfortable high-speed rail (with family-friendly facilities like playgrounds on board, so that all travellers can enjoy the experience) and new sleeper train networks to connect continents. The Night Sprinter network is a proposed grid of night trains to connect Europe using 40 international long-distance lines, with the aim of connecting more than 200 cities. The cooperatively owned European Sleeper, a Dutch–Belgian railway founded in 2021, makes some of this reality: it connects to the Eurostar to take travellers to Berlin, Dresden and Prague, and has ambitions to expand to southern Europe and Scandinavia.

In the US, the largest investment in public rail since the creation of Amtrak was announced in 2023, with US$66 billion allocated, including to high-speed rail projects that will be open from 2028. China's high-speed rail network, which is viewed as world-class, stands at 45,000 kilometres and will increase to 65,000 kilometres by 2035.[39]

Long-term increases in cycle paths and a wave of design innovation in e-bikes and cargo bikes are convincing more people to swap their cars for active transport on a daily basis. A cargo bike, with its storage room, is a viable alternative to a second car – or any car – particularly for families transporting children to school or biking to do the weekly food shop. E-bikes have been outselling electric cars in the US and UK, while in Germany, the bicycle market quadrupled from 2012 to 2022, with e-bikes making up 48% of the market.[40] Research from the University of Auckland has found that cyclists are the happiest commuters due to four factors: the reliability of the journey, the sensory stimulation, the feel-good effects of exercising outdoors and the increased opportunities for social interaction.[41] A longitudinal study published in 2023 found that cycling orients people 'towards the common good';[42] the US Department of Transportation invested US$3 billion in 2024 into projects supporting walking, cycling and public transport in communities specifically for community reconnection and repair.

Policies can work quickly to normalise new ideas, and behavioural change is very powerful. Many people took up active mobility during the pandemic, and as the effects of air pollution become starker, cities increasingly want to become less car-dependent. It's worth remembering that both cars and the reorganisation of our built environments to revolve around them are relatively recent developments – traffic lights are just over 150 years old – yet they have entirely reshaped our mental infrastructure about the way things should be. Initiatives like walking buses and bike buses – school- and community-organised groups of people who walk, wheel or cycle together en masse – could radically change how we inhabit and design our public spaces in future.

Like more-than-human futures, degrowth requires not only a political and financial commitment but that we, as individuals and societies, take on a very different way of thinking. Growth is not only an economic principle, it is built into how we see personal trajectories around work (over time, we will gain more skills, more experience, more responsibility and therefore more money) and at home (over time, we will buy a house, buy a bigger car, go on more luxurious holidays). Growth is built into our language and the expressions we use: it informs our world view at the most fundamental level.

To go against economic growth is to go against the grain, but every successful counterculture has taken on a system that seemed, at the time, unchangeable. The momentum around degrowth as a future vision – even when the word itself is not used – is steadily growing across political, economic and industrial strategy, and the broader idea of living less individually and more collectively is increasingly resonant with people. While some of the central theory feels removed from everyday relevance and experience, the overall goal – of rebalancing wellbeing and wealth, and replacing consumerism with creativity and community – is finding a wide and engaged audience.

3
Solarpunk

'We believe solar is the most natural and humane source of energy. It's the answer to the smaller question (How to power our life?) and the Big one (How to live it?)... This world has questions. We should desire and design new answers. Always sunny side up.'

From the manifesto of the Solar Movement,
an initiative by solar designers Marjan van
Aubel and Pauline van Dongen[1]

Solarpunk is a literary, aesthetic and cultural genre that portrays an equitable society sustained by renewable energy and living in harmony with nature. It was developed to offer an appealing climate future, or 'the best possible Anthropocene'.[2] Solarpunk has been proposed as a successor to steampunk and dieselpunk, aesthetics that pay tribute to previous energy ages, but it's most often framed as an alternative to cyberpunk, the dystopian literary genre that emerged in the 1980s. Its founding purpose, as stated in the Solarpunk Manifesto, is to answer and embody the question, 'What does a sustainable civilisation look like, and how can we get there?'[3]

Where cyberpunk exists in a dark urban setting, in shadows and rain, illuminated by the glare of advertisement screens, neon signs or car lights, solarpunk lives in full daylight, powered by the sun, glowing with life, and living lightly. Where cyberpunk is coolly critical of the power systems it operates within, solarpunk is warmly hopeful that it can dismantle them and create something new. Amazofuturism, Afrofuturism, biophilic design and traditional crafts are recurring visual and cultural references. Technology is often central to solarpunk imagery, and is innovative and advanced, but developed to be ecologically integrated, equitable and ethical. Solarpunk is often utopian: luminous, decorative and verdant. It's also radically human: researcher Adam Flynn, who wrote several of the foundational texts of solarpunk and co-administrates the website solarpunks.net, has summarised it as 'a future with a human face and dirt behind its ears'.[4] Jay Springett, a strategist and fellow solarpunks.net co-administrator who helped popularise the movement, has emphasised that solarpunk imagery should always include people. Solarpunk is not only about solar energy, but the sun does carry a symbolic significance. If society takes on the world view of the energy it uses, fossil fuel's extractive damage will be replaced by solar power's renewable light, which will change not only how we power our buildings and manufacturing, but how we design and organise our cultures.

Solarpunk was born online in the mid-2000s. One of the earliest uses of the word is in a 2008 post on a WordPress blog called Republic of the Bees, and it was disseminated gradually and organically across early social networks, including Tumblr blogs. The idea was in the air: several people described the overarching concept of solarpunk in the 2010s, only to discover that a term capturing their ideas already existed. In 2012, a Brazilian science-fiction anthology called *Solarpunk: Ecological and Fantastic Stories in a Sustainable World* was published; an English translation followed in 2018. Adam Flynn's article 'Solarpunk: notes toward a manifesto' was published on the Project Hieroglyph website in 2014, presenting a rallying cry against green consumerism and doomsday narratives and stating that, 'We're solarpunks because the only other options are denial or despair.'[5]

Responding to a period of history where people were feeling ecological anxiety and struggling to think hopefully about their future, solarpunk quickly found a receptive audience among writers, thinkers, makers and artists. The original aesthetics of solarpunk, particularly those proposed by Tumblr user missolivialouise in an early and widely shared post,[6] included Art Nouveau, artisan trades, stained-glass solar panels, and a serene green cityscape by digital artist Imperial Boy (Teikoku Shônen). Decorative and textured, they offered an intentional alternative to the smooth, white, geometric and futuristic tech objects that were proliferating at the time, such as the iPod. The aesthetic keywords that were listed were mixed in with advances in technology (solar rooftops! Airships!) and social and political changes (education in tech and food growing! Less corporate capitalism!), showing how solarpunk has always been a mix of aesthetic and creative, and political and social, in its intent. The aesthetics of solarpunk have broadened and varied considerably since then, and are continuously evolving. Speaking on a podcast in 2023, Justine Norton-Kertson, founder and editor-in-chief of *Solarpunk Magazine*, said, 'We don't want to pigeonhole solarpunk as only one thing; that compartmentalising... is going to prevent solarpunk from reaching more people.'[7]

Solarpunk has been envisioned from the start as a movement as much as an aesthetic. This is a strategic decision, of which Flynn has written, 'we need banners to rally around, and there is power in forming subcultures around ideas.'[8] The politics at the core of solarpunk are anti-capitalist, decolonial, anti-racist and feminist, and the movement sees humans achieving social as well as technological progression. It's this rebellion and resistance against current power structures, including pessimism around the future, that earns the movement its -punk suffix. Although the look of solarpunk can seem cosy and even quaint, it presents a radically alternative way of living, one that includes gender liberation, equality and diversity as core values.

Springett describes the movement as a container and a memetic engine, and one of the benefits of this approach is that the result is polyphonic. The community that has grown around it – in part because it was born and developed through participatory online mediums like Tumblr – maintains a culture of discussion, debate and respect for multiple perspectives. That being said, the people who are most visible across solarpunk's foundational writing are often white men, and because anyone can add creative inspirations to the container, projects can be claimed as solarpunk without their creators intending them to be or even knowing that they have been.

Writer Rhys Williams has critiqued the movement for an 'underlying whiteness' and for invoking 'the fascism of utopia'.[9] Solarpunk can seem so hopeful that an observer may wonder: where is the unappealing stuff, what is done with it? Who isn't welcome in this place, and what happens to them? Writer and critic Paul Graham Raven has written about its 'unbearable lightness', describing solarpunk as 'less an alternative to the present paradigm than a best-case extrapolation of it'.[10] It's been called 'the Hufflepuff of punks' and 'the lovechild of hippies and futurists'.[11] Solarpunk walks a fine line between twee and subversive, and it's criticised for being both too radical and not radical enough. This has made its increased influence on culture over the past few years all the more interesting.

Solarpunk has thrived on blogs and mood boards and in literature, particularly in independent and small-press publishing; there are multiple solarpunk anthologies, several solarpunk novels and a magazine devoted to it.[12] Around the turn of the decade, solarpunk started to move off the mood boards to influence wider media. The depiction of Wakanda, the African city featured in the film *Black Panther* in 2018, was a joyful moment for solarpunks, showing how a civilisation could combine the benefits of cutting-edge technology with living in balance with its environment. Other depictions of solarpunk ideals have been more complicated, particularly as they have started to be commercialised and co-opted by brands. In 2021, yogurt company Chobani released an animated advert that showed a solarpunk society in detail: in the future pastoral, a multigenerational family eat locally harvested food against a backdrop of floating wind turbines, green skyscrapers, a flying school bus and orange-picking robots. A decommodified edit of the advert was swiftly released online by solarpunks, removing all of the brand references.

In the same year, Nike released an advert called 'Play New: Tomorrow'. In it, a domed greenhouse is populated with workers in white lab coats, who are watering plants that grow into furry sneakers. 'Oh man, I want those!' cries the voice-over. 'When are these dropping?'

The next year, solarpunk was Disneyfied. The film *Strange World* tells the story of a progressive civilisation that is powered by a plant called 'Pando' – a stand-in for fossil fuels – and must transition away from using it. With a multigenerational and diverse group of characters and a collaborative and radically hopeful perspective on bringing about change, the film carries many solarpunk ideas. It performed poorly at the box office, making a loss for Disney, and unlike the Chobani advert, hasn't been widely folded into solarpunk canon.

Alongside films and advertisements, solarpunk's themes are increasingly present in gaming. Like books and films, games provide an attractive way into solarpunk ideas, creating immersive worlds to bring them to life and make them interactive, and sometimes sparking an interest that the player can then start to explore outside of the game. A calm survival game called *Solarpunk* was successfully funded on Kickstarter in 2023, and features rural homesteading, transparent computer screens and high-tech airships. It's joined by *Terra Nil*, an environmental strategy game in which players bring life to a barren landscape by cleaning up oceans, planting trees and reintroducing wildlife, then leave. *Loftia*, created by Qloud Games, focuses on cosy themes of farming and crafting, and raised over US$1.2 million on Kickstarter. Daybreak, a cooperative board game in which players use social, political and technological tools to stop climate change, came out in the same year.

Solarpunk also got a big political endorsement in 2023, when US Representative Alexandria Ocasio-Cortez stated on a social media feed that she ascribes to solarpunk instead of climate doomerism.[13] This brought new fans to the movement, and new critics.

As it graduates from a marginal internet subculture to a bigger movement with growing influence, solarpunk is necessarily becoming more real – louder, more confident and less aesthetically idealised. The combination of natural systems, social action and high-tech ingenuity that it aims for is increasingly being prototyped at a range of scales. The open question is whether a movement that started online and is decentralised and largely unmanaged can transition to real-world applications without losing its guiding principles, its aesthetic appeal and its progressive and anti-capitalist centre. Can a subcultural future vision remain intact as it becomes a stronger influence on mainstream culture? Or will it have achieved its purpose if it is subsumed, meaning that its ideas have been taken up on a mass level and are making a positive difference on a global scale – even if they've been adapted along the way?

DIY NETWORKS

Solarpunk celebrates and finds great value in DIY, hacked and bolted-together solutions, which might have been invented and developed by individuals or together by communities of makers, fixers and planters. This 'let's try it' approach is mushrooming today, in services and products ranging from home-made internet services to locally networked energy and backyard bioreactors.

As people begin to reclaim the spaces and processes immediately available to them, new tools and products are being developed to help them become more self-sufficient and climate-conscious in the choices they are making. Wildgrid is a practical, action-based education platform that guides people through decarbonising their home, covering heat pumps; the installation of solar panels and induction stoves; insulation and plumbing;

and the US tax rebates available for each. The platform is gently gamified, offering 'quests' to encourage people to increase their activities and gradually become more confident in moving from bite-sized adjustments to big changes. 'Climate is such a scary and anxiety-inducing subject, I think everything we can do to make it easier to understand and more enjoyable will make more people want to join in,' says co-founder and CEO Krystal Persaud.[14]

Circular solutions to make homesteads more fully self-sufficient are being developed. Designer Rebecca Schedler created Symbiopunk, a mechanical bioreactor and composting system that turns human faeces into organic fertiliser – suitable for use in gardens or on farms – using mycelium to break down the waste. While Symbiopunk was a one-off project, a waterless compost toilet system was launched by Swedish brand Harvest Moon at Stockholm Design Week 2024. Called Luna, the toilet has been developed to be comfortable, stylish and user-friendly while making water-free toilets an everyday normality as people look to save energy, use less water, and integrate closed-loop reuse systems into their homes. The Biosphere Cellulose Kitchen, a speculative prototype developed by US-based designer Abi Lambert, brings similar ideas to material preparation. The kitchen unit integrates simple production facilities for making bacterial cellulose, envisioning a future where people can ferment, wash and dry their own cellulose as a home-made alternative to single-use plastic.

While these examples require significant commitment, the pathway to experimenting with DIY lifestyles has been significantly broadened by the public information networks that platforms like YouTube and Instructables have created. Easy-to-watch videos break down topics like backyard aquaponics into step-by-step tutorials on how to set up and maintain these systems in a way as simple as looking after a goldfish. Simple programming tools and open-source kits and components enable hobbyist DIYers to rig up proactive home systems, such as smart lighting that responds to national weather alerts, changing colour to indicate an incoming storm. Equipped with enthusiasm and a small amount of knowledge, beginner solarpunks can then find online communities to help them troubleshoot and learn as they go.

Peer-to-peer tools, created by individual makers and then shared with wider groups or channels, are also enabling hobbyists to quickly scale up their ambitions. American computer programmer Darius Kazemi has released 'Run your own social', a guide to making very small social media networks aimed at programmers and non-programmers alike, while acknowledging that running your own social media network is a significant undertaking.

Solarpunks see themselves firmly as the product of a networked society and are not rejecting technology or digital communications, but they are rethinking how these systems can and should operate. There is a lot of enthusiasm for technology in solarpunk circles, but also an awareness that it should be used appropriately, creatively and for social good.

Community tech is increasingly appealing and attainable to solarpunks and beyond. Cheaper components and real-time digital organising tools have helped encourage people to take utilities and basic commons services away from big companies and put them into the hands of volunteers, communities and grassroots networks.

Supported by donations and run by volunteers, NYC Mesh is a community mesh network that aims to provide open, free and reliable connectivity to New Yorkers, maximising access rather than profits, and without tracking users or collecting personal data. Grassroots community mesh networks started to gain more attention in the US during the pandemic as the realities of the country's digital divide became very apparent. Networks such as Philly Community Wireless were launched during this time, but there are active examples in operation around the world. Guifi.net, in rural Catalonia, is the largest: started in 2004, it now serves more than 100,000 people as a commons, using 40,000 nodes. These networks will only become more relevant as climate breakdown causes more frequent disasters and extreme weather events, making intermittent connectivity an increasingly normal occurrence. Operating on a human scale and distributed across many nodes, mesh networks can offer high resilience during disasters, because there is no single point of failure. They come with all the challenges of volunteer-based organising, including oscillating levels of momentum, consensus and funding, but when they work, they can create a positive impact for the long term.

A similar wave of distributed innovation is taking place in renewable energy, where community-owned models offer the potential not only to transition our energy sources, but to redesign how we access, own and distribute power sources.

Localised mixes of approaches and large-scale, citywide initiatives are emerging, making energy a much more civic project in which people can take ownership and feel pride. The shift from being a consumer to being a producer is immediately empowering, and energy independence can quickly build togetherness. Italian architect Carlo Ratti has envisaged self-powered spaces in which a range of renewable energies – including small wind turbines, photovoltaic panels, a vibraphone that converts music into electricity, and a carousel that is powered by the children who play on it – all contribute to community generation. US-based mini hydropower company Emrgy places turbines in irrigation canals, each generating enough power to sustain a small neighbourhood. In Liverpool in the UK, the local authority is planning Mersey Tidal Power, a tidal barrage system that would be fitted along the River Mersey to generate clean energy for the entire city for the next 120 years, while also providing flood defences for the city as climate change worsens.

Beautiful new designs are changing how renewables look, bringing a more decorative approach – sometimes incidentally, sometimes purposefully – to the infrastructure that will soon reshape our built environment. Airloom Energy's wind turbines look almost sculptural, like alien artefacts transplanted into terrestrial landscapes. Their unusual design enables them to function at less than one-tenth of the cost of a standard turbine and to have a lower profile. Australian company Diffuse Energy's plug-and-play wind turbines can be used for microgrids and employ diffusers to encircle the blades of the turbine and double their energy production. As a result, they resemble small hand fans that can fit to existing towers. If energy infrastructure becomes smaller-scale, distributed and localised, we could see many more of these creative and innovative ideas emerging to bring a more varied aesthetic to our visual experience of the green transition.

Solarpunks are interested in the reimagined societal structures and energy justice that could be made possible by all types of renewable power, including wind and hydro. But it's solar power that inspired the movement's name, and it's solar power that tends to most capture the public imagination. As the world heats, solarpunks envisage a photon-powered society emerging, in which not only our energy production but also the rhythms of our lives follow the sun and its light.

SOLARISED THINKING

Solarpunk revolves around a central vision of abundant solar power – and thanks to better and cheaper panels and battery storage, that vision is firmly within sight today. Solar energy is now the fastest-growing energy technology in history. In 2022, wind and solar supplied 22% of Europe's electricity, overtaking gas (at 20%) for the first time.[15] By 2023, solar alone accounted for 15.8% of Brazil's energy mix, coming second to hydroelectric plants (49%); globally, renewable sources provided a record 30% of electricity generation that year.[16] In 2024, wind and solar made up 40% of China's installed power generation capacity, edging ahead of coal (at 37%) for the first time.[17] In Australia, nearly one in three homes now have rooftop solar, which provides 11% of the country's electricity.[18] As of 2023, the

IEA reported that manufacturing capacity for solar photovoltaics and batteries was on track to meet its Net Zero Emissions by 2050 Scenario.[19]

The scale of installation and pace of innovation within solar energy are dizzying, and the promise and potential of a world that is energised by solar is quickly coming to life. We are becoming used to seeing solar panels fitted to rooftops, but increasingly they will be fitted into our environment in much more dynamic ways. Photovoltaic facades could be used to dress buildings in solar textiles, while seas and lakes could be scattered with floatovoltaics: floating circles of solar panels that follow the sun to increase their efficiency while cooling the water and helping to prevent algal bloom.

Mobile solar is changing transport: German company Sono Motors fits solar technology to vehicles including buses, trucks and recreational vehicles, and has developed solar panels that can be integrated almost invisibly onto the doors of cars. Toyota's next-generation Prius can be fitted with solar panels on its roof, which charge the car's battery while it's parked.

One of the breakthrough technologies at tech industry trade show CES in 2024 was photovoltaics the size of a postage stamp. Made by a company called Ambient Photonics, they charge from minimal levels of ambient light, which means that everyday devices that use relatively little energy – like sensors, keyboards and headphones – could run entirely on ambiently gathered solar energy, requiring no batteries and little maintenance. This opens up the possibility of installing ubiquitous, ambient and autonomous sensors into environments to perform functions such as biomonitoring – monitoring natural ecosystems for significant changes, such as increased pollution or disrupted air quality.

Solar panels are increasingly being combined with other systems and uses, creating compound benefits. Placed over car parks, they bring energy generation directly into urban areas, where energy is likely to be used in higher quantities, including by the EVs parked underneath; placed over canals, they can reduce excess evaporation. Hanging solar panels over crops of tomato and jalapeño plants has been found to increase the yield of the plants substantially, reduce water use and increase the output of the solar panels. Used with greenhouses, solar panels can extend growing seasons and increase crop yields. Photovoltaic farms can also be designed to be pollinator-friendly, encouraging biodiversity by growing wildflower meadows amid the panels. At Arnold Arboretum in Massachusetts, horticulturalists have observed birds nesting beneath the solar panels, and they say the solar farm is humming with insect life.

The Solar Manifesto, by solar designers Marjan van Aubel and Pauline van Dongen, calls for designers to expand the material aesthetics of solar energy. 'Part of our job is to find new ways to wrap it in,' they write. 'Let's make the technology colorful, soft, cuddly, pliable, invisible, modular, full of playful patterns.' The designers have worked energetically and creatively to bring solar energy into cultural contexts, including organising the Solar Biennale in the Netherlands in 2022. According to the Solar Manifesto, 'With solar design, there's the potential to add energy to just about any material, surface, or object.'[20]

One of the earliest aesthetic suggestions made for solarpunk was stained-glass solar panels, an idea that has been developed by designers but not yet scaled up. The energy technology is compatible with artisanal aesthetics and production, though, and this interplay is being explored by artists and designers. Yuca_tech, a community-based project in Yucatán by Mexican artist Amor Muñoz, looked at combining local crafts with technology, including a series of photovoltaic textile panels that incorporate traditional fibres and weaving techniques. Italian company Dyaqua has developed artisan-made textured clay roof tiles that house silicon cells under the ceramic, so that cultural heritage buildings can be fitted with solar panels that do not disrupt their traditional appearance.

Alongside the innovation and creativity that solar energy inspires, and the changes it brings to how we design our world, it will also necessitate some changes to how we live. Despite the continued record growth rate of renewable energy, fossil fuels continue to provide more than 80% of the world's primary energy consumption, and carbon dioxide emissions from energy reached a record high of 34.4 billion metric tons in 2023.[21] Demand for oil continues to grow. The rapid rise of renewables has largely been providing an energy addition rather than an energy transition. It also brings with it significant material challenges. Recycling is increasingly being implemented for the materials required to produce clean energy infrastructure, such as solar panels, but extraction of the metals and minerals needed to enable clean energy is still going to surge. Benchmark Mineral Intelligence forecasts that by 2040, one month's worth of lithium needs will be equivalent to all of the battery-grade lithium produced in 2021.[22] To truly switch to renewables, and to minimise the damage inflicted by mining the materials they need to function, we'll need to reduce overall energy use and change the rhythms with which we live.

Writer and solarpunk advocate Andrew Dana Hudson has described the idea of a photon-powered society that is organised around high-tech days and low-tech nights, where people plan activities for when energy supply is plentiful and reduce activity when it's not going to be available. Dutch designer Boudewijn

Buitenhek took this idea to an extreme with his Living with the Sun project. He conducted an experiment in which he lived without gas and electricity for a week, only using power he was able to generate himself – from a flexible solar panel that he could move around his balcony and a pedal-powered generator – to 'observe the consequences it had' on his life. 'I believed I had prepared myself,' he told me by email, 'but I still feel like I underestimated how much I would miss a hot or cold drink or food of any kind. My kitchen was mostly useless, as my stove, microwave and fridge all far exceeded the energy I could collect from the sun.' To make himself a cup of coffee, he built a solar-powered water boiler and coffee roaster, and moved his coffee time from the morning to the afternoon to enable him to roast the beans and heat the water effectively in time. 'It led me to ponder potential future implications for property value being more closely linked to sunlight accessibility,' he said. Since the experiment ended, he has installed a solar panel and battery that enable him to watch a couple of hours of solar-powered TV each day. 'It still brings me joy when I see the battery fully charged in the evening.'

Digital experiences will need to be redesigned to follow the sun. Solar Protocol is a website powered by a network of solar-powered servers. Developed by three artists and technologists – Tega Brain, Alex Nathanson and Benedetta Piantella – it explores the question, 'Could we subvert modernist dreams of designing machines to control our environments and instead let our environments control our machines?'[23] When you visit the website, a short text and compass-like illustration explain which server is currently sending it to you.

At a more mainstream level, tools are emerging that enable people to switch their routines and make different choices according to the energy mix available to them throughout the day. In 2023, Apple introduced Grid Forecast, a feature on its Home app that highlights when renewable energy will be available to use over the day ahead. The feature can help people decide when to embark on high-energy activities such as charging their car or putting a wash on, offering a simple and undemanding way to start to reconfigure daily routines to be energy-centred.

Solarpunk futures explore what it could mean to live within the sun's beams, but they also entail becoming more entangled with nature as a whole. Technology is integrated into the environment in creative ways – and as climate breakdown becomes more advanced, direct action to alter the environment is becoming more of a talking point.

RADICAL NATURE

Solarpunk visions of nature are less about skyscrapers covered in plants and more about urban gardens, compost systems and algae biopanels. In short, they're less clean and green, more messy and experimental – but often equally cutting-edge.

Seed bombs, guerrilla gardening and permablitzing – focused one-day events in which volunteers conduct permaculture-related activities such as creating a food garden, constructing a grey-water system or planting trees – have been recurring themes through the solarpunk movement's decade-plus of ideas gathering. In the UK, a growing network of groups called Incredible Edible is pushing for a Right to Grow law, which would require local authorities to map out all of the public land suitable for use in community cultivation, such as food gardens. The move could open up a wave of grassroots regreening. Brazilian skydiver Luigi Cani took the idea of radical regreening to new heights in 2022, when he engaged in seedbombing the Amazon. Cani skydived into a deforested area of the rainforest, carrying a box containing 100 million seeds from 27 native plants to disperse.

Other projects are combining nature with technology to create cutting-edge concepts that draw on living intelligence. Mexican company Greenfluidics produces window panels that are filled with water rich in algae, fed by carbon dioxide emissions, to shade buildings while producing a source of biofuel to power them. Light Bio engineers bioluminescent plants using genetic enhancement. Its first product, the Firefly Petunia, has the soft glow of moonlight and became commercially available in 2024, making it possible for gardens to be naturally illuminated after dark.

Natural intelligence is also informing how information is stored and how computers could be built – or grown – in future. Biotech company Grow Your Own Cloud is developing ways to store data in the DNA of plants. It has prototyped data gardens that sequester carbon while storing kilobytes of information, such as an image file; its future visions include forests that double as data archives for petabytes of data. Bristol-based Unconventional Computing Laboratory has conducted feasibility studies of fungal computers, in which mycelium forms part of an electronic circuit and can receive and send electrical signals. The lab has also developed kombucha electronics, made by printing dried kombucha mats with simple circuit boards, which could pave the way for future bio-wearable devices that are literally home-brewed.

Propelled by climate necessity and a spirit of invention, innovators are developing contraptions and inventions that stabilise water supplies, monitor pollution levels and automate food production. Canadian company Oneka Technologies' floating desalination machines are powered by the movements of the waves, drawing in seawater and pumping it to land as fresh drinking water. Operating entirely mechanically, the machines are relatively small-scale – the largest is eight metres by five metres – and can be fitted in waves that are just one metre high. As more areas become affected by water stress, defined as when demand for water outstrips available local supply, these machines could become staples for coastal populations.

As depicted in the solarpunk Chobani advert, robots are a common sight within solarpunk futures, and they are likely to be used for a range of service and maintenance roles as their deployment becomes cheaper and more accessible. US start-up farm-ng has developed a series of modular farming robots that growers can build, Lego-like, at low cost, customising the robot according to the type of crop and task, such as weeding, seeding and spreading compost. German company Nature Robots uses AI and robotics to assist regenerative and small-scale farming specifically. Its autonomous robot can navigate forests and tunnels, and capture three-dimensional (3D) maps of plants as it works. Australian company Hullbot makes an underwater drone that autonomously inspects, maps and cleans the hulls of marine vessels, reducing the environmental impact of boats by, among other things, minimising the risk of transferring invasive species into waters.

Robots that actively restore and regenerate environments could be the next stage. Dubai-based designer Mazyar Etehadi has designed A'seedbot, a robot that tackles desertification by identifying fertile areas of barren land and planting seeds based on data from its sensors and navigation.

UK not-for-profit company Real Ice aims to preserve and restore Arctic sea ice, to prevent the tipping point that will occur as part of climate breakdown if it disappears. The company frames replacing sea ice as analogous to planting trees, in that it is a climate solution critical to the years ahead. It hopes to develop an underwater drone that can measure the thickness of ice, pump up water, refuel, and progress to the next area to repeat the process, creating a scalable solution that would ultimately be managed locally by Indigenous communities. As well as being a type of direct action – and one that feels distinctly more radical than planting trees – Arctic ice refreezing is a form of geoengineering. Defined as a deliberate, large-scale manipulation of an environmental process, geoengineering is a topic that divides opinion among solarpunks, climate scientists, policymakers and beyond, and is fast becoming central to futures discussions.

Some people see geoengineering as a crucial tool to undo the damage that humans have done to the climate, and argue that it is worth developing these processes to the point that we understand more of their consequences and can deploy them relatively responsibly at scale. The counterargument is that geoengineering is a dangerous distraction from proven climate solutions, papering over the symptoms of the problem rather than fixing it, and will provide a licence for the continued extraction of fossil fuels, eradication of biodiversity, and emission of pollution.

As climate breakdown becomes more visible and more extreme, geoengineering is becoming more appealing, despite its risks. In 2023, three of the co-founders of activist group Extinction Rebellion wrote in favour of 'experimenting with marine cloud brightening in the Arctic and exploring every option for climate restoration and cooling'.[24] Around the same time, a group of more than 400 scientists published a letter petitioning for responsible R&D of ocean-based carbon dioxide removal methods, such as ocean alkalinity enhancement.

Speculative architect Liam Young's film *The Great Endeavour* explores the idea of installing carbon removal infrastructure on a planetary scale. Young has spoken about the need to update our environmental ideals, making the point that the small-scale, individual and community action that has played a large role in environmental activism for decades is not enough to address the level of environmental breakdown that has now occurred. As the scale of the problem has grown, he argues, the scale of the solutions also needs to grow.[25]

While this debate is happening, and well before global consensus has been reached, geoengineering is starting to be deployed. At the moment, it is often happening on a small and experimental scale, as activists and mavericks attempt to re-engineer nature, on their own, in a bid to reverse climate change.

In 2012, 100 tonnes of iron sulphate were deposited into the Pacific Ocean by a DIY geoengineer aiming to fertilise the ocean by stimulating the growth of phytoplankton that absorb carbon dioxide. Although its full effects can't be measured, it proved to be a mostly harmless act and may have worked: the deposit created a significant algal bloom and was followed by a record salmon harvest the following year.

Since 2022, the company Make Sunsets has been deploying small-scale stratospheric aerosol injection, a way to cool the planet by sending balloons filled with sulphur dioxide into the stratosphere to create reflective clouds that send the sun's rays back into space. The company sells cooling credits to customers, which function like carbon offset credits, and also offers DIY kits so that anyone can make and release their own balloons.

This punk phase of geoengineering experiments is likely to be short-lived, as investment is beginning to pour into the sector, formalising and scaling up projects.

Frontier is an advance market commitment that aims to guarantee future demand for carbon removal by committing US$1 billion to it between 2022 and 2030. Founded by tech companies including Alphabet, Meta and Stripe, Frontier has contracted more than 200,000 tons of carbon removal from more than 30 projects involving surface mineralisation, ocean alkalinity enhancement, geologic mineralisation, enhanced weathering and direct ocean removal. These include a start-up called Lithos Carbon, which has received US$57 million – Frontier's biggest commitment to date – to remove 154,000 tons of carbon dioxide over the next four years. Lithos works with farmers in the US to spread crushed rock across fields, which reacts with rainfall to capture carbon dioxide, which will then eventually make its way into the ocean and be sequestered. The process, called enhanced weathering, can also increase yields for farmers and works in months rather than years. Its speed and scalability make it an attractive proposition for organisations looking to quickly reduce their environmental impact.

Solarpunk as an aesthetic and as a movement examines how we will get to a sustainable future, but it also devotes its energy to imagining and illustrating what that future will be like to live in. This worldbuilding is essential to motivate and inspire people to change the choices they make today, and to thread action today through to future benefits. It's crucial as a way to tell stories of hope and prosperity, even in anxious times.

JOYFUL ALTERNATIVES

The imagination that powers solarpunk, coupled with its premise of radical hope, makes it an energising and uplifting movement to spend time with. Plenty of the ideas and projects contained within solarpunk are not strictly necessary, but are inventive and pleasing and perhaps slightly strange; when people make things for themselves, these are often the kinds of things that they make.

Researcher Eric Hunting has mapped out the near, mid- and far future of a possible solarpunk society in an in-depth, illustrated essay on post-industrial design and aesthetics, published on Medium in 2020.[26] In the early stages of a solarpunk future, he envisages wide-ranging and divergent applications of creativity as people start to make more things for themselves and their community: 'Tiny Houses, earthen architecture, and funky repurposed vehicles and buildings. CNC/laser cut plywood and rediscovered DIY "hippie" furniture made from recyclables… A vast menagerie of quirky homebrew and human-powered vehicles.'

Solarpunk not only has room for rational production of necessary items, but makes space for pleasure and enjoyment, even hedonism. Artist Olalekan Jeyifous's architectural concepts, such as Aeroponic Roof Garden, Bed-Stuy Urban Bubble Farm and Rooftop Rainwater Harvest, are visualisations of urban interventions that make it possible to live more communally and agriculturally within a city by claiming rooftops or unused pockets of space. Assembled largely from found components and reused parts, their colourful and joyful design makes them look like fairground rides or creative industrial salvage, and they are a way of generating excitement around alternative stories about how we might live.

Transport is one area in which the more playful and exuberant side of solarpunk lifestyles shines through particularly brightly. Airships are a recurring motif through solarpunk fiction and media, tapping into a visual vocabulary of lightness and airiness that also includes sail-powered boats and kites. Instead of feeling restrictive or frugal, these modes of transport feel fun and recreational, and open up new types of leisure experiences.

UK-based company Hybrid Air Vehicles builds four types of airships, called Airlanders, which it intends to produce as electric, zero-emissions vehicles from 2030. Its first hybrid airship is set to enter commercial use in 2028 and will be used by French tour operator Grands Espaces for voyages to the Arctic region. Because the airship can take off from any flat surface, including ice, its destinations can reach beyond those possible for other aircraft, opening up extraordinary travel experiences. With space for up to 100 passengers and a top speed of 130 km/h, the airships will have spacious, relaxed interiors that resemble lounges, with plump chairs and chaises longues, bar seating and floor-to-ceiling windows.

The leisure opportunity for travel by airship is enticing, but there's also significant potential in using airships to deliver humanitarian aid, care supplies and cargo such as timber or wind turbine components to areas where this type of transport is uniquely positioned to reach. Several companies, including Hybrid Air Vehicles, are exploring this idea. 'The world's open for us to rethink what we do by air,' says CEO Tom Grundy.[27]

The next generation of airships, if they take off, will revive a form of transport that was last popular 100 years ago. Other projects are giving new momentum to boats, using high-tech variants on a much older technology: sails. Mitsubishi's Pyxis Ocean ship completed a six-month voyage in 2023, equipped with WindWings sails, which reduced the fuel use of the ship by 3 tonnes a day, rising to 11 tonnes in optimum sailing conditions. Following the trial, WindWings producer BAR Technologies now plans to roll out production globally.

Swedish company Oceanbird's wind propulsion sails work similarly and have a strikingly designed opening mechanism: they unfurl from lying flat on top of the ship in a movement that looks like a bird opening its wings after a doze. They also reduce underwater sound pollution, removing noise disruptive to animals such as whales, who share space with boats. EcoClipper, a cooperatively owned Dutch start-up, is decarbonising transport using more traditional sails. The start-up's clipper ships carry cargo and passengers, and began commercial sailing in 2023. The company hopes to operate a fleet of 25 ships in future.

Argentinian artist Tomás Saraceno has been experimenting with creating a hot-air balloon powered by wind and sun for years. In 2020, his 'aerosolar'-powered art piece Aerocene Pacha set multiple records flying over the Salinas Grandes salt flats in Argentina, drawing strategic attention to a bioregion being targeted for lithium mining against the wishes of local communities. The one-person balloon's debut flight marks the first time humans have flown freely, without using batteries, lithium, solar panels, helium or hydrogen. The balloon carried the message 'Water and Life are Worth More than Lithium'.

The penultimate line in the Solarpunk Manifesto is that solarpunk 'is beautiful', and it's these projects – the ideas that not only show what we could do to repair ecology and improve our societies, but also illustrate the experiences in which we will find pleasure, meaning and excitement – that bring solarpunk to life to its fullest.

Solarpunk bridges the aesthetic, cultural and political spheres, creating an all-encompassing set of stories and ideas around how to create and inhabit a hopeful, inclusive and radically liveable future. It has gained traction across creative culture over the past decade, and is the first future vision to be born online and grow to a considerable size and level of influence. It came at the right time, and is answering a series of questions that more and more people are asking. If it continues to gain momentum, its future impact is likely to be wide-ranging and often subtle, to the point where it will be difficult to track a cohesive through line. But that, to some solarpunks if not all, will be a triumph: if solarpunk becomes the default, it has succeeded.

4
Metaverse

'What we're dealing with here is not just a technology, it's also an artistic medium: something that can be used to create new types of experiences that we've never seen before.'

Keiichi Matsuda, director of XR design studio
Liquid City, speaking at SXSW in 2024[1]

The metaverse is a technological concept that describes a global network of large-scale, live and interactive virtual worlds that people can inhabit together. Proposed as a successor to the current internet, it's sometimes called the Spatial Web or the embodied internet. Matthew Ball, the technology analyst and investor who published an influential nine-part series of essays sketching out the metaverse, defines it as 'a massively scaled and interoperable network of real-time rendered 3D virtual worlds'.[2] It is a permanent although continuously changing space, and it is connected to the economy, so that people can make and spend money within it. The conditions needed for the metaverse to exist have been anticipated for decades, and include a confluence of technologies and behaviours that are all now in place: global digital connectivity, high-speed real-time graphic rendering and processing, the mainstream adoption of personal computers, and the social normalisation of spending time in a virtual world for a range of reasons, including work, socialising and entertainment.

In the technology industry, engineers and technologists are often deeply inspired by science fiction, devoting their life's work to creating products and experiences that have been envisioned by writers, sometimes decades earlier. This is the case with the metaverse, which has featured in countless sci-fi depictions across novels, TV and film under a variety of names and guises. Science-fiction writer Vernor Vinge explored 'the other plane' in 1981,[3] and William Gibson introduced 'cyberspace' in 1982,[4] both using terms that frame virtual experiences as spaces with dimensionality. Neal Stephenson coined the word 'metaverse' in his 1992 novel *Snow Crash*, which directly inspired the founders of Roblox and Epic (the maker of Fortnite).

Ernest Cline branded his virtual world the OASIS in *Ready Player One* in 2011; copies of the book were handed out to employees at VR company Oculus when they joined.[5]

VR has a long history and is arguably one of the tech industry's oldest and most established visions of the future. Its roots in the Silicon Valley canon stretch over many decades of R&D. The first VR headset, the 'Stereoscopic-television apparatus for individual use', looks remarkably like the headsets available today; inventor Morton Heilig filed the patent for it in 1957 and was granted it in 1960. Research has continued ever since, and the field has become known as extended reality (XR) – an umbrella term that includes augmented reality (AR), mixed reality (MR) and VR. Technologist Jaron Lanier popularised the term VR in the late 1980s.[6]

One of the biggest open questions around the metaverse is what we'll do in it that will lead to the killer app: the use case that is important or convenient or exciting enough to bring about mainstream adoption of what is still a fairly niche set of technologies.

Many of the early applications and goals of people working in VR were to augment the human; to make humans 'better' by enabling us to use more of our senses, enhance our empathy or access more information or tools at once, and to train and upskill people more quickly. VR was an experimental area of research, and entertainment and media applications started to emerge. Nicole Stenger created the immersive VR movie *Angels* from 1989 to 1991, and Nonny de la Peña introduced walk-around VR in 2012 with the immersive journalism documentary *Hunger in Los Angeles*. VR experiences have helped researchers understand the pre-adaptation of the human body: we are remarkably capable of adapting to new limbs, or controlling a tail; we are very quickly able to assume the world view of another person or animal, and it can be thrilling – and deeply affecting – to do so.

There are plenty of people and companies still working on immersive XR experiences and on utility-driven applications of AR and MR. The metaverse is distinct to these applications. It is more often seen as a social and shared experience: technologies such as spatial computing or VR are what will create the metaverse, but they are not the end result. The metaverse is a place or, more accurately, a network of places. It is inhabitable: one of the ideas that sets the metaverse apart from the internet of the early 2000s is 'presence', the feeling of being there and, beyond that, 'co-presence' – the feeling of being with other people. The headsets or large immersive screens we use to enter the metaverse make it a head-up experience, rather than the head down and sunken shoulders that typify using a smartphone. The metaverse is something to be part of, rather than to look at. And this makes it a space, a physical experience that needs to be understood and designed.

As architectural practice Space Popular has explained, 'Our everyday lives are already overlaid by a multitude of digital augmentations and interactions. Immersive technology gives a third dimension to an already existing virtual layer. This means that what used to be an issue of graphics and two-dimensional design, is now an issue of spatial design, architecture and urbanism.'[7]

Virtual worlds have existed as social and communal spaces since at least the 1980s: *Habitat*, a large-scale virtual community, was created in 1985 and available to inhabit from 1986 to 1988. It has since been revived and rebuilt in various versions. *Second Life*, a 3D online world developed by Linden Lab, was launched in 2003 and captured both the public and the media's imagination for a short period by offering a rich and fully functioning society in which people could make a full-time living digitally and create their own culture and norms. *Second Life* had more than a million monthly active users at its peak in 2007; as of 2023, it was attracting around 750,000 users.

Games engines like Unity and Unreal Engine can now be used to make much more advanced and visually sophisticated spaces and people (often known as avatars). Massive multiplayer games and games platforms, such as Fortnite and Roblox, have been characterised as early metaverses and are very popular: Fortnite hit a high of 11.6 million concurrent players in December 2023, while Roblox had 71.5 million daily active users at the end of 2023. Corporations that have built their names on worldbuilding, such as Disney, are investing heavily in building out branded digital worlds, often within these already popular spaces.

In terms of media coverage and investment, the metaverse has had a rapid rise and dizzying descent in this decade alone. In 2021, it was the idea of the moment for the tech industry; by the next year, the industry had moved on to the next big thing, and the metaverse's moment had passed. But the tech industry is still betting big on it for the long term and continues to invest heavily in the metaverse's foundation technology: hardware and software, AI-powered tools and systems, chips and compute, and display technologies. And while some companies, thought leaders and news outlets have moved on, other people, businesses and governments are still very interested in the metaverse. As with other digital ideas, systems and tools – like contactless payment, QR codes and cryptocurrency – different countries will adopt, encourage, reject or regulate the idea of the metaverse at different paces and at different levels. Japan established the Japan Metaverse Economic Zone, with support from technology companies including Fujitsu and Mitsubishi, in early 2023; later that year, China's Ministry of Industry and Information Technology announced the Three-Year Action Plan for the Industrial Innovation and Development of the Metaverse (2023–2025).

In terms of its current trajectory, the metaverse is the most business-as-usual future that features in this book. We expect advances in technology to change how we live; this is a narrative that people are generally comfortable with. Numerous experts have pointed out that the metaverse exists today, and the worldmaking is already happening. Wagner James Au, author of *Making a Metaverse That Matters* and founder of metaverse news and culture website New World Notes, told me, 'The greatest misconception about the metaverse is that it's a vague, faraway concept without a clear definition – or worse, that it's a mere marketing buzzword.'

The futures we've explored so far in this book all revolve around adapting to having less – if more is measured solely in stuff. In the metaverse, this is tantalisingly untrue, although the 'more' we enjoy will all be digitally rendered. This sense of abundance extends to language: in his essay newsletter *The Convivial Society*, L.M. Sacasas writes, 'While language tethered to the material world appears to diminish, language tethered to the virtual realm endlessly proliferates and fragments.'[8]

Presented as a world of endless possibilities, it's easy to see how the metaverse offers an appealing vision of more creativity, more prosperity, more freedom. Like all future visions, part of its messaging comes from real hope and excitement and possibility – and part of it is pure hype. The metaverse is a perfect case study of the hype cycle in action.

HYPE CYCLE FUTURES

One of the curious traditions of the tech industry, and particularly of Silicon Valley, is its adherence to a chart that determines which tech is hot and which is not. Introduced in 1995 by American IT consultancy Gartner, the Gartner Hype Cycle assesses the maturity and adoption of emerging technologies and places them into one of five positions, which are represented graphically on a chart. When a technology is invented, it enters the chart at its first point, the 'innovation trigger'; it then rises up to the 'peak of inflated expectations', dips down into the 'trough of disillusionment', carries on up the 'slope of enlightenment' and eventually hits the 'plateau of productivity', which signals mainstream adoption. This five-point model has been highly influential to the tech industry, and while the chart itself has become less prominent over time, the hype cycle's terms are still commonly used in conversation to diagnose the current status and perception of a technology. Alongside this, technologies are described as going through broader seasonal cycles: summers – where investment is significant, breakthroughs are happening and interest is high – and winters, where investment dries up, commercial applications recede and interest decreases. In short, the expectation in tech development is that the highs will be high and the lows will be low. Partly as a result of these framings, technological future visions are often overhyped, both in their success and in their failure. Both have happened with the metaverse, and before that with VR, in remarkably condensed periods of time.

The development of VR began in the 1960s and experienced periods of hype in the 1980s and 1990s, as the technology hit an interesting point, and books and films were released that created wider public interest in it. *Tron* captured imaginations in 1982. William Gibson's short story 'Burning Chrome', which effectively set off the cyberpunk genre, was published in the same year; Neal Stephenson's novel *Snow Crash* appeared a decade later. Each time, the technology was not ready for consumer use, and culture moved on.

The early 2000s saw another mini-wave, particularly around virtual spaces such as *Second Life*, as personal computers became more common and people again began to think and dream about what they could do digitally. But reality didn't live up to expectation for many, and computers had other, more immediately useful purposes.

By 2012, a major piece of the puzzle had fallen into place. Computing had advanced, and with it a global supply chain of components, to the point that it was possible to build specialised hardware. In some sci-fi depictions of the metaverse, participants need to place electrodes onto their brain, or be implanted with electronic devices that become part of their body. In others, virtual worlds are experienced as intentional hallucinations, which are accessed by drugs or by other stimulations of the mind. But the metaverse is most commonly entered via a headset – a helmet, goggles or glasses. This headset arrived, to widespread excitement across the tech industry, in the form of the Oculus Rift.

Oculus's headset delivered the vision of VR that films had promised – or close enough to it – and a wave of smartphone-based VR headsets followed from companies including Samsung and Google. Facebook acquired Oculus in 2014 and continued developing its technology and launching new headsets, which were mainly promoted and used for gaming. By 2020, the tech industry was facing a backlash in media coverage and public perception: social media had begun to be seen as a more negative force than previously, government regulation was coming, and a new opportunity was needed.

Against this backdrop, the Covid-19 pandemic began. People were stuck at home and looking for entertainment, driving a boom in gaming and online socialising, and spurring mainstream adoption of proto-metaverse experiences. At this time, the word 'metaverse' started to be used more frequently across the technology sector and the creative industries. By late 2021, Facebook had changed its name to Meta, announced tens of billions of dollars of investment in building the metaverse and ushered the idea of an immersive virtual future into the mainstream.

From 2021 to 2022, the hype around the metaverse was off the charts. The central narrative was that the metaverse was coming, it would change everything and people would effectively live there. Buying metaverse 'real estate' was described as a forward-thinking investment decision by Tokens.com CEO Andrew Kiguel,[9] akin to buying property in Manhattan in the 18th century; Coca-Cola even launched a special-edition metaverse-inspired drink called Byte. With so much pressure on the metaverse, the hype bubble started to wobble, and by 2023, company earnings calls and layoffs of metaverse-focused teams indicated that businesses had not seen the immediate customer interest that they had hoped for.

Technology journalist Casey Newton has thoughtfully framed this very condensed hype cycle as 'the year-long discussion we had about the metaverse from 2021 to 2022'.[10] The upshot of this discussion, broadly speaking, was that hype needs to be backed up by genuine use cases – reasons that people might want to access and participate in virtual worlds, consistently, for the long term. But the backlash was as inflated as the hype, and even as the metaverse fell into the trough of disillusionment, the industry held out hope that the arrival of Apple's long-rumoured MR headset could revive it. (Researcher David Karpf has described VR headsets as 'the rich white kid of technology',[11] as they are always lauded for their potential and given more chances to succeed.)

In June 2023, Apple announced the Vision Pro, a cutting-edge headset that it noticeably avoided ever associating with the words 'VR' and 'metaverse', describing it instead as 'spatial computing'. Introducing a number of innovative features and functions, including holographic-looking 'personas' and an interface controlled by a combination of eye-tracking and hand-tracking, it was declared to be 'the Northstar the VR industry needed, whether we admit it or not' by Hugo Barra, former head of Oculus.[12]

It's at the point when technologies enter the downward slope in the hype cycle, and investment and media attention fall away, that they can become the most interesting. R&D continues, on a smaller, scrappier scale that attracts people with passion and curiosity, rather than people who can sense the possibility of making easy money. Over the next 10 years, there are likely to be more winters and more summers for the idea of the metaverse, with peaks and troughs of interest, and the tech that makes it possible consistently developing throughout, until it reaches the point where it may be a viable mainstream consumer option. Introduced to social gaming throughout their childhood by way of popular platforms like Roblox and Minecraft, people in their tweens and teens today will grow up as virtual natives who are comfortable with the idea of the metaverse, even while they aim to balance their overall reliance on technology. As of 2024, 33% of teens in the US owned a VR device, according to investment bank Piper Sandler's semi-annual survey.[13]

Even at its highest point, there was a limit to how long most people envisaged themselves spending in the metaverse. A 2022 McKinsey survey, conducted at the peak of the hype cycle, found that US consumers expected to spend about 3.7 hours a day in the metaverse by 2027.[14]

In the UK, people spend 13 hours a day looking at screens, and 92% of people multiscreen.[15] Spending time in the metaverse might not mean adding yet more screen time, as it would probably replace existing online activities. But by using screens more intensely and to the point of total immersion – closing our field of view and replacing it either substantially or entirely with digital layers – we will be, for better or worse, choosing a different reality. And if we are to continue the public discussion we have had about the metaverse, we'll need to consider the implications.

REALITY PRIVILEGE

In a 2021 interview with writer Niccolo Soldo, US tech investor Marc Andreessen argued that while some people enjoy 'reality privilege' – their life is beautiful, stimulating and filled with interesting and desirable people – the majority of people lack it, and their online world will be far superior to their offline world.[16] This statement was quickly picked up by metaverse advocates, who argued that the metaverse could act as a democratising force for wondrous experiences – making it possible for anyone to visit Machu Picchu digitally, for example – and enable digital equality, even while physical inequality remains.

The metaverse enables people to remake reality. This could have positive consequences – like visiting far-off locations that would otherwise be out of reach for all but the richest people – but equally, it could enable us to individualise our experiences even more than we already do. Deep Reality, a project developed by the MIT Fluid Interfaces group, is an interactive VR experience that uses biofeedback from the user – measured via a headset and wristband – to determine the visuals and other sensory elements (pulses of light, movement, sound) that they are exposed to. These elements are designed to gradually relax the user, progressively changing their state of mind. In Deep Reality, the outcome of such a tailored and personal experience is positive and beautiful. In other settings, individualised virtual experiences could cause us to lose shared ground and become more divided as a society. The unifying cultural moments that we still have could be replaced by highly personalised experiences that we can't share.

One of the most chilling depictions of personalised realities I have seen showed an escalator of people, all of whose faces had been replaced in real time by smiling emojis as they went past. The Artvertiser, a project developed by Julian Oliver, Damian Stewart and Arturo Castro from 2008 onwards, is an AR software program that detects advertising billboards in the user's field of view and automatically replaces them with pieces of art. One of the benefits of having an editable view is that you can adjust the colour contrast, zoom into images or text, have text read aloud and create countless other custom features that will increase accessibility for people with disabilities. As virtual layers are added to our world view, reality can be edited for many purposes, some of which we will like, and some of which we won't.

Early studies have found that extended use of VR can blur the distinctions between what has happened virtually and what has happened in the physical world. A 2009 study found that after using immersive virtual environment technologies, some children exhibited false memories drawn from watching avatars perform actions.[17] A 2014 self-experiment by Frank Steinicke, Professor of Human–Computer Interaction at the University of Hamburg, found that during 24 hours of intensive use of VR, he 'mixed certain artefacts and events between both worlds' and exhibited confusion about which he was in.[18] Extended use of headsets has also been linked to feelings of unreality. A 2024 study by 11 researchers from Stanford University and Michigan State University investigated the psychological implications of wearing an MR headset in public and seeing the world through pass-through video technology. 'In our field notes,' the authors write, 'social absence was common – people in the real world simply felt less real... Being in public could sometimes feel more like watching TV than interacting face-to-face.'[19]

Critics argue that the tech companies who have already diminished our capability to be present in the real world – by increasing our reliance on screens and devices – are now selling us a better future in a fully synthetic world. Some of the early reviews of the Apple Vision Pro supported this hypothesis, with writers noting how flat and disappointing they found the real world after they had removed the headset.

Prolonged use of XR headsets is associated with computer vision syndrome, a condition that includes eye irritation, blurred vision and headaches. VR headsets frequently trigger nausea, particularly for women, who experience 'simulator sickness' with 40% higher intensity than men.[20] Gendered differences continue into the experiences that the headsets enable: women are sexually harassed in VR spaces to the extent that some platforms have introduced measures such as safety bubbles and mute and block functions to give users options to keep harassers away. In a 2018 survey of more than 600 regular users of social VR platforms, 49% of women had experienced at least one instance of sexual harassment.[21] On-screen assaults feel real – and as hardware developments such as haptics make the sensorial experience of virtual spaces more convincing, the verisimilitude will only increase.

The metaverse doesn't have to be entered via a headset. Many proto-metaverses can be accessed fully via a laptop, and they are increasingly available via smartphone. Eventually, the technology needed to port someone into a virtual world could move off their body and into the space around them. Technology companies are developing interactive projectors, haptic flooring systems that recreate textures and sensations virtually using pressure and vibration, and immersive set-ups in which the person's movements and expressions are tracked by the room around them, rather than by wearables. These projects are expensive and unscaled, for now, but they could give the metaverse broader appeal over time. They could also sharpen the divide between people with access to more advanced and immersive hardware, who would be able to experience virtual worlds at their fullest, and people accessing the metaverse via a less powerful computer set-up, who would experience a reduced version.

As with any future vision, it's important to consider who is promoting this image of the future, and why. Who will own and operate the metaverse; should it be one company or any company? Who has the right, the power or the privilege to define its parameters? Who processes and stores the data that needs to be collected for the metaverse to function, and what are their motives? These questions are increasingly pressing: researchers have found that commercially available headsets already collect enough data during their use that machine learning models can predict the wearer's weight, height, age, ethnicity and marital status with 70–80% accuracy.[22]

In an article written for *MIT Technology Review* in 2022, cybernetics scholar Genevieve Bell drew a line connecting the worldmaking activities of the Great Exhibition and World's Fairs, and the worldmaking of the metaverse in the early 2020s.[23] It's a prescient reminder that humans have made worlds before, many times, and that technological innovation has a long history of being used to distract from oppression and inequity. Given the power to remake reality, what will we make?

CO-CREATED WORLDS

Digital artist Krista Kim has called the metaverse 'the greatest art project in human history'.[24] This perspective chimes with some of the earliest visions that VR developers had for their field. The first generation of commercial VR products aimed to encourage free-form creativity and invention with tools that would enable groups of people to create together, as if they were playing music. The freedom and excitement that unspooled in the early days of VR development reflected the fact that it's quite simply very fun to design your own world – instantly, fluidly, together – and then to redesign it, seconds later, when your mood or need changes. Where centralised ideas of virtual spaces developed by large corporations have struggled to find a foothold, smaller creative outputs continue to thrive, and they often do so by celebrating this spirit of experimentation and co-creation.

The maker-spaces of today's metaverse are made up of lots of miniverses, which together start to paint a picture of what a DIY, open-source virtual world could look like and how it could function. No-code platform Yahaha invites anyone to create 3D environments and games to hang out in with their friends; *Rec Room* works in a similar way. Rooms is a more lo-fi 3D room-making app that essentially focuses on interior design; players create a room and publish it for others to explore. The homepage for Rooms shows a honeycomb of rooms that have already been designed, stretching out seemingly into infinity and showcasing the expansive creativity that has already been let loose.

Advances in generative AI are lowering the barrier to entry further, and making more sophisticated world-making available to beginners – in some cases, only text prompts are needed to generate environments. In the same way that platforms such as WordPress and Squarespace made it possible for non-experts to design and launch a blog or website, next-gen metaverse-making platforms will make virtual world creation accessible to anyone who is interested and has access to the internet.

Miniverses serve a range of purposes, but most revolve around casual socialising and gaming. As they grow, and as the internet is reorganised into a network of places to visit, these destinations will gradually begin to offer their own, more specialised ambience and host a wider range of experiences. Digital fashion entrepreneur Karinna Grant told me that one of the aspects of the metaverse she's excited about is '3D shopping environments', which could shake up the way we shop online now into something that's much more social, interactive and engaging. Social experiences can also extend to mass virtual concerts, housing thousands or even millions of participants at once, as well as activism and awareness-raising. While people may be unable or unwilling to protest in physical spaces, for example, virtual protests are increasingly common on proto-metaverse platforms.

For some people, the anonymity and pseudonymity that the metaverse affords is freeing. They can depict themselves as they want to be seen, avoiding stereotyping or unwelcome assumptions, and they experience far less social anxiety as a result. For marginalised groups in particular, accurate representation is deeply important. In a 2021 report by the Institute of Digital Fashion, 87% of respondents said that their digital identities coordinate with their IRL (in real life) identity.[25] 'I always seek to represent myself as there is barely any visibility for Black women digitally,' said one focus group respondent. The survey found that 92% of people want customisation options for their avatars and that 60% stick closely to their regular fashion style when dressing their avatar, while 40% choose to dress in a more 'surreal' style.

More than 10 million of Roblox's daily active users changed their avatar every day in 2022, and flexibility of self-expression has already become a cornerstone of metaverse experiences. More recently, the game has added the ability for people to change their physical appearance while they are playing – by adding freckles or altering the shape of their jaw, for example. While some of these decisions may seem trivial, the avatars that people embody in virtual worlds have measurable consequences: researcher Nick Yee's studies in gaming have found that when players use a more attractive avatar, they act with more confidence.[26] Social media filters have already changed how people perceive their own attractiveness, creating a converged idea of beauty that has been called 'Instagram face'. It's possible that as avatars influence aesthetic expectations, beauty standards will narrow even further, driving people to undergo cosmetic treatments to better resemble their virtual selves. It's also possible that the aesthetics of the metaverse will diverge and become more diverse, sparking new creative movements and making space for a broader range of styles and tastes.

As the technology powering the metaverse becomes more advanced, the visual possibilities of digital design will expand beyond the cartoon-like imagery that recurs today. In 2024, Roblox announced Texture Generator, which is able to 'skin' objects, such as draping and wooden joints, with realistic contouring and 3D material effects. Simulated fabrics can look worn and patinated, and effects such as embroidery can be rendered in more realistic detail. These capabilities make it possible for designers to use more artisanal and sensorial materials and styles, which could help to expand the metaverse aesthetic beyond the shiny, cyber and futuristic looks that digital fashion is often associated with. This would widen the appeal of digital design, entice more artists to begin to create inside – and for – virtual spaces, and in turn attract more people to use them.

Designers are also thinking about the ways in which we could enter, exit and traverse the metaverse. What happens to the process of clicking a hyperlink and opening a new web page in an internet that is embodied? Architectural practice Space Popular has spent time considering portals and how to create a welcoming transition into and between virtual spaces. One of its answers takes the form of draped virtual textiles that are pulled aside like curtains, providing a tactile gateway into a new space. Software design company STRV has developed a meditation experience for the Apple Vision Pro, called *Float*, which similarly designs an intentional transition between physical and virtual: reality is gradually softened until the wearer of the headset finds themselves in fully virtual surroundings. As the user experience of the metaverse develops, its architects will be able to draw from visual perception, body language, hand gestures and even dance to inform the way people use and navigate virtual space.

This diversity and elasticity of experience extends to spatial design. Andreea Ion Cojocaru is the CEO and co-founder of NUMENA, developer of the VR game *The Third Pill*. In one of the levels of the game, the floor shrinks you as you walk across it. 'Space is not equally distributed on this floor,' she told me. 'Moments like that create experiences you will never have in physical reality but that feel incredible in VR.'

When I asked what digital spaces offer that physical spaces might lack, and about the creative possibilities of the metaverse, digital designer and artist Lucy Hardcastle told me: 'The virtual or the digital has more layers of reality to it, or more potential layers, in terms of storytelling, creating an experience. The things that stand out to me are being able to play with physics or sensory elements, or creating visual magic that isn't possible in an IRL experience. With the digital, there's potential to access a deeper level of immersion.' For designers, architects and culture-makers, the metaverse offers a near-infinite canvas and a paintbox that has yet to be unpacked.

Hardcastle also noted that 'the digital is easier for a user to escape within'. The word 'escape' is prevalent across discussions around VR and the metaverse. The obvious question this elicits is: what are we escaping from? In almost all of the science-fiction depictions of the internet of the future, the answer is clear: when the virtual is thriving, the real world is decidedly not.

THE NATUREVERSE

Switching physical activities for virtual replacements is often touted as a way to reduce greenhouse gas emissions and overall environmental impact. The paperless office envisaged a complete replacement of paper correspondence with less resource-intensive emails; working from home every day instead of commuting to an office has been estimated to reduce emissions by up to 54% according to a 2023 study by Cornell University and Microsoft.[27] (People have to commit, though; hybrid working with one day a week at home lowers emissions by only 2%.) By replacing a significant number of objects and activities with virtual versions – a process that is known as dematerialisation – the metaverse is positioned to continue this trend.

Digital fashion, in particular, is framed as a way to continue purchasing and enjoying clothes without contributing to textile or packaging waste, using thousands of litres of water to manufacture items, or shipping them around the world. According to DRESSX, a leading digital fashion marketplace, producing a digital garment emits 97% less CO_2 than producing a physical garment. If a digital purchase does not replace a physical purchase one-to-one, though, the benefits will be wiped out. Instead of altering consumption patterns, a rise in digital fashion could serve to accelerate them by acting as a gateway to buying physical fashion or functioning as an additional purchase for customers – effectively a second, virtual wardrobe – on top of the physical clothing they already buy. Digital clothing itself is also not as low-impact as it might seem because of the significant environmental impact of the data centres and ICT infrastructure required to create, process, sell and store it – along with every other part of the metaverse.

According to a 2024 report by the IEA, data centres used an estimated 460 TWh of electricity in 2022, making up almost 2% of global electricity usage.[28] That amount is expected to double over the next two years; a functioning metaverse would be likely to send electricity use skyrocketing. Running an immersive, compelling and globally available metaverse, in real time and without lag, will require a significantly higher amount of computing power than is available today.

Data centres also use large amounts of water, as the computer systems they house heat up and have to be continuously cooled to function, and many are located in water-stressed areas. As droughts become more common, so do protests from local communities and representatives, who point out the irresponsibility of allocating millions of gallons of water to computers when people and crops need it. Tech companies are developing ways to mitigate water use – for example, by placing data centres in the sea, as China has done off the coast of Sanya – but these solutions tend to encroach further on the environment, replacing one problem with another.[29]

The relationship between the ascension of the digital and the descent of the natural is striking in its symmetry. As more space is given to computers, less space is apportioned to wildlife. As biodiversity has decreased, our time spent indoors and on screens has increased. And as the physical world becomes denatured, virtual worlds are blooming with depictions of imagined, enhanced and idealised natural aesthetics. *Headspace XR*, an experience that became available on Meta's Quest 3 headset in 2024, places people in a virtual landscape to meditate, walk and spend time with friends. It features soft pink hills, red trees, bubbling water and an abundance of hanging plants.

Artist Refik Anadol's immersive audiovisual experiences apply AI tools to natural inputs. Using the Large Nature Model, which is trained on a data set of 500 million images of nature, including audio and visual data collected from 16 rainforest locations by Anadol's studio, the artist fills gallery walls with AI-generated visualisations of flowers and fungi, creating immersive and constantly changing artworks that are difficult to look away from.

Digital nature can be impossibly smooth, glossy, vivid and shape-shifting; even at its most experimental, it usually appears pristine. This version of nature feels more comfortable for people who have grown up not in wild environments, but viewing them through glass, and it is fast becoming the version of nature we are more accustomed to experiencing.

The attraction that artists feel to creating virtual renditions of nature is not necessarily misplaced: viewing images of nature has been linked to improved mood. A study published in 2015 found that participants who were shown photos of green outdoor spaces (parks, gardens and fields) after being submitted to a stressful experience started to calm down more quickly than those who were shown photos of the built environment (cars, buildings and roads).[30]

Virtual experiences that centre nature could play a part in bringing about a heightened appreciation of ecology, encouraging people to preserve and protect it. In digital artist Alice Bucknell's game *The Alluvials*, players take on multiple more-than-human perspectives throughout, including in one level playing as wildfire, and in another alternating between the symbiotic roles of tree and moth. Hyphen-Labs' project *[AR]boreal Servers* uses AR to digitally reforest a street with memories, which take the form of sculptures decorated with leaves and flowers.

In some cases, digitised recreations will replace their real-world equivalents. The Pacific island country of Tuvalu sits just above water level; its inhabitants are already witnessing land being claimed by the rising sea, and by 2100 it is likely to be uninhabitable, making it one of the first countries to be lost to climate breakdown. To preserve its culture, geography, history and state sovereignty, it is creating a backup copy of itself that can continue to function even as its people disperse around the world. Tuvalu's three coral islands and six atolls are being captured by satellite images, photos and drone footage to create a detailed digital twin that can preserve, for its digital diaspora, what is disappearing in reality.

Jaron Lanier has said that the best part of virtual experiences is the moment when you take off the headset and attune again to the wonders of reality.[31] The metaverse is a heady technological vision that promises a new dimension of experience, social interaction and self-identity. If it's designed well, and used in balanced doses, it has the potential to add value to the lives of billions of people, for a wide range of reasons, and in many different contexts. To the virtual natives growing up today, it is likely to be the logical next stage in the evolution of how we live, as the digital and physical become ever more seamlessly fused. To some people, it sounds like the least appealing idea possible – and it probably always will. But whatever the outcome, and to whatever extent the metaverse does come to be part of our futures, the hope should remain that we won't need a virtual world to wholly escape to – and that we can also regenerate, reimagine and redesign our physical reality.

Call to Action: How to Think into Futures – Tools and Thought-Starters

Together we have explored four possible futures. If you would like to think further into any of these futures – or into another possible future – here are six exercises or approaches you could use to do so. They can be used alone or in a group, and you can mix and match them as you wish.

PERFORM A CRITICAL EVALUATION

Make a list of the key ideas, developments or future visions you want to evaluate. Then ask these questions:

- Who is promoting a future or a concept, and what do they stand to gain from its adoption?
- Who is included in this future, and who is excluded or ignored?
- Who would or could be harmed by this future?
- What problems does it solve? What problems might it create?
- Look at your answers. Do they skew positive or negative, or is there a mix? How do you feel about this future overall now that you have examined it more closely?

ANALYSE ACROSS SECTORS

To stress-test how feasible or strong a future vision is, analyse how many areas it is being influenced by or emerging from. A strong, probable or preferable future is likely to be present across each of these areas:

- Social
- Political/Economic
- Technological
- Environmental
- Cultural and Literary*

* 'Literary' doesn't feature in conventional STEEP or PESTLE methodologies but is very helpful for futures thinking: the most compelling futures often see an uptick in fiction being written about them.

MAP AND CHANGE THE AXES OF FOCUS

Plot the futures you are analysing within different axes of focus. You could place 'nature' and 'technology' as two ends of one axis, and 'community' and 'corporate' as two ends of the other axis, for example. You could also use your own words.

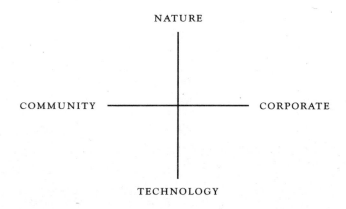

Within the four quadrants produced by these two axes, map the futures you are thinking about and move them around to provoke fresh ways of thinking and imagining.

- For example: if a very nature-focused future vision moves into the technological quadrant, how would that change it? What new benefits, challenges or harms might it bring about?
- Similarly, if a community-focused future were to become commercialised by a company, how would that change it?

WRITE EVOCATIVE SCENARIOS

Scenarios are short stories that paint a picture of a future, sometimes from a particular character's point of view. They can be useful to bring an idea to life and make it more relatable by filling in everyday details or specifics.

For example:

- What does a morning routine look like in this future?
- What toothpaste does your character use?
- How does your character get to work, and what job do they do?
- How do they socialise or take part in their community?
- What are their priorities and aspirations – what matters most to them?

Scenarios are one of the most popular ways to summarise futures, as they can be used to easily compare and contrast a range of future trajectories. They very clearly make the point that there is not one future, and that numerous options always exist. They are often used in government and corporate futures thinking projects.

For examples of scenarios developed by professional futures thinkers, look up Institute for the Future (https://www.iftf.org).

CREATE FUTURE ARTEFACTS

Designers and makers can benefit from prototyping items that may exist or be needed in a future vision.

By making futures tangible in the form of products or artefacts, we can better understand what the consequences of those futures might be. These hypothetical objects pair well with scenarios, making futures able to be physically played with.

You can create a brief or assignment for a future artefact by outlining the basic parameters of that future, such as:

- What materials are available in this future?
- What does this item do, and who will be using it?
- Why does it need to exist?

From the four futures we looked at in this book, we could ask:

- What would a map look like in a more-than-human future?
- What would you find in a home that has been designed around the ideas of degrowth?
- How would a solarpunk smartphone look and feel?
- What kind of experiences would be advertised in the metaverse, and how?

For examples of design artefacts that have been made by professional futures thinkers, look up work by The Near Future Laboratory (https://nearfuturelaboratory.com) or Superflux (https://superflux.in/).

PURSUE PREFERRED FUTURES

This last exercise is crucial.

- Map the futures you want, and create a plan of how you could start to bring them into being.
- Localise and personalise your preferred futures, combining and reassembling the ideas that you believe will improve society.
- Make them relevant and beneficial to your community and possible within your spheres of influence.
- Talk about them to everyone. Then start to make them happen.

Notes

AN INTRODUCTION TO FUTURES

1. Bruce Sterling, 'The singularity: your future as a black hole', Long Now seminar, 11 June 2004.
2. William Gibson, interview on *Today*, BBC Radio 4, 20 January 2020.
3. McCourtney Institute for Democracy at Penn State University, 'Mood of the nation poll', December 2021.
4. YouGov, 'Has the pandemic changed views on human extinction?', 16 February 2022.
5. Caroline Hickman, Elizabeth Marks, Panu Pihkala, et al., 'Climate anxiety in children and young people and their beliefs about government response to climate change: a global survey', *The Lancet*, 5(12), pp. e863–e873, December 2021.
6. Rebecca Solnit, '"If you win the popular imagination, you change the game": why we need new stories on climate', *The Guardian*, 12 January 2023.
7. Phoebe Tickell, 'New Deep Narratives: we need new stories of what it means to be human', Culture Hack Labs, 11 April 2022.
8. Bill McKibben, 'The Climate Crisis', *The New Yorker*, 9 June 2021.
9. Martin E.P. Seligman, Peter Railton, Roy F. Baumeister, et al., 'Navigating into the future or driven by the past', *Perspectives on Psychological Science*, 8(2), pp. 119–141, 2013.

10 Adam Mastroianni and Ethan Ludwin-Peery, 'Things could be better', PsyArXiv Preprints, 14 November 2022.
11 Donella Meadows, 'Envisioning a sustainable world', Third Biennial Meeting of the International Society for Ecological Economics, 24–28 October 1994.
12 Ruha Benjamin, *Race After Technology: Abolitionist Tools for the New Jim Code* (Polity, 2019).
13 Caroline Criado Perez, *Invisible Women: Exposing Data Bias in a World Designed for Men* (Vintage, 2019).
14 Kevin Kelly, 'Protopia', *The Technium*, 19 May 2011.
15 Monika Bielskyte, 'PROTOPIA FUTURES [FRAMEWORK]', Medium, 18 May 2021.
16 UNESCO, 'Futures Literacy', 2012 onwards.

I. MORE-THAN-HUMAN

1 Kim Stanley Robinson interview in Klaus Æ Mogensen, 'Mars is irrelevant to us now. We should of course concentrate on maintaining the habitability of the Earth', *Farsight*, 10 August 2022.
2 Alison Abbott, 'Scientists bust myth that our bodies have more bacteria than human cells', *Nature*, 8 January 2016.
3 'New Zealand's Whanganui River granted legal status as a person after 170-year battle', ABC News, 15 March 2017.
4 Chloe Berge, 'This Canadian river is now legally a person. It's not the only one', *National Geographic*, 15 April 2022.
5 Nicholas Bryner, 'Colombian Supreme Court recognizes rights of the Amazon River ecosystem', IUCN, 20 April 2018.
6 Jonathan Moens, 'See the beautiful, ecologically priceless trees Italy is protecting forever', *National Geographic*, 8 September 2021.
7 Annie Evans, 'Animal Welfare (Sentience) Act formally recognises animals as sentient beings', World Animal Protection, 6 May 2022.

8 'France drafts "ecocide" bill to punish acts of environmental damage', France24, 17 April 2021.
9 Maïthé Chini, 'Belgium becomes first in EU to recognise ecocide as international crime', *The Brussels Times*, 23 February 2024.
10 Pella Thiel, 'Rights of the forest – Rules for a wild relationship', pellathiel.se, 11 September 2020.
11 Carolina Conti, '"We are digital guerrilla fighters": Q&A with young Indigenous activist Samela Sateré Mawé', Mongabay, 23 December 2022.
12 Enrique Salmón, 'Kincentric ecology: Indigenous perceptions of the human–nature relationship', *Ecological Applications*, 10(5), pp. 1327–1332, 2000.
13 Casper A. Hallman, Martin Sorg, Eelke Jongejans, et al., 'More than 75 percent decline over 27 years in total flying insect biomass in protected areas', *PLOS One* 12(10), 18 October 2017.
14 Lior Greenspoon, Eyal Krieger, Ron Sender, et al., 'The global biomass of wild mammals', *PNAS* 120(10), 27 February 2023.
15 Nat Barker, 'Es Devlin creates indoor forest as venue for COP26 events', *Dezeen*, 9 November 2021.
16 Naomi Rea, 'Olafur Eliasson hauls 30 icebergs to London, inviting the public to contemplate the devastating effects of climate change', Artnet, 11 December 2018.
17 Oli Stratford, 'Enter the zoöp', *Disegno*, 19 May 2022.
18 Spencer Feingold, 'How artificial intelligence is helping us decode animal languages', World Economic Forum, 5 January 2023.
19 Briana Abrahms, Neil H. Carter, T.J. Clark-Wolf, et al., 'Climate change as a global amplifier of human-wildlife conflict', *Nature Climate Change*, 13, pp. 224–234, 2023.
20 'ECOncrete's co-founders on reconnecting to nature and finding inspiration for revitalizing marine ecosystems (part 1)', Biomimicry Institute, 31 August 2020.

21 Tate, 'Magdalena Abakanowicz: A Timeline', 17 November 2022.
22 Anab Jain, 'Calling for a more-than-human politics', Medium, 19 February 2020.
23 https://pauseandeffect.ca.
24 Janine Benyus, '2022 Bicentenary Medal Event', RSA YouTube, 16 December 2022.
25 Marcus Fairs, '"I'm not an enormous advocate of planting trees" says Sebastian Cox', Dezeen, 2 July 2020.
26 Indigenous Protocol and Artificial Intelligence Working Group, indigenous-ai.net, 2019–2020.
27 Dorion Sagan and Lynn Margulis, 'Gaia and the evolution of machines', *Whole Earth Review*, 55, pp. 15–21, Summer 1987.
28 Warren Ellis, 'Future fields: WILDING, Isabella Tree', Warren Ellis Ltd, 10 August 2022.
29 'Four in five Britons support rewilding, poll finds', Rewilding Britain Press Hub, 19 January 2022.
30 Damian Carrington, 'Two-hour "dose" of nature significantly boosts health – study', *The Guardian*, 13 June 2019.
31 Patrick Barkham, '"I'm glowing": scientists are unlocking secrets of why forests make us happy', *The Guardian*, 2 September 2022.
32 Philip Oldfield, '"We must do better than 1,000 Trees"', Dezeen, 14 January 2022.
33 Shakara Tyler, 'Farming out loud', *RSA Journal*, 27 June 2022.
34 flocktogether.world, Instagram.
35 Meredith Evans, 'Becoming sensor in the Planthroposcene: an interview with Natasha Myers', Visual and New Media Review, *Fieldsights*, 9 July 2020.
36 'Most consumers in western Europe want alternatives to conventional meat, survey shows', Good Food Institute Europe, 22 September 2022.
37 Lauren Nardella, 'Meat consumption holds steady as consumers alter amount, type to combat inflation', FoodNavigator USA, 24 March 2023.

38 Earthling Ed (Ed Winters), Instagram, 4 April 2023.
39 Natasha Myers, 'How to grow liveable worlds: ten (not-so-easy) steps for life in the Planthroposcene', ABC, 6 January 2021.

2. DEGROWTH

1 Patrik Svensson and Rebecca Tamás, 'In conversation: Patrik Svensson & Rebecca Tamás', *Granta*, 23 April 2021.
2 John Stuart Mill, 'Of the Stationary State', *Principles of Political Economy*, Book IV, Chapter VI (1848).
3 Emily Stewart, 'What GDP does and doesn't tell us', Vox, 28 July 2022.
4 Rebecca Riddell, Nabil Ahmed, Alex Maitland, et al., 'Inequality Inc. How corporate power divides our world and the need for a new era of public action', Oxfam, 15 January 2024.
5 Torsten Grothmann, Vivian Frick, Richard Harnisch, et al., 'Umweltbewusstsein in Deutschland 2022', German Environment Agency, August 2023.
6 Lily Paulson and Milena Büchs, 'Public acceptance of post-growth: factors and implications for post-growth strategy', *Futures*, 143, October 2022.
7 'New polling shows ongoing support for socialism among young Britons', Institute of Economic Affairs, 9 March 2023.
8 'Nearly three quarters of millionaires polled in G20 countries support higher taxes on wealth, over half think extreme wealth is a "threat to democracy"', Patriotic Millionaires UK, 16 January 2024.
9 Martin Sandbu, '"Degrowth" starts to move in from Europe's policy fringes', *Financial Times*, 30 May 2023.
10 Jason Hickel, 'Degrowth is about global justice', *Green European Journal*, 5 January 2022.
11 For 74%, see Jason Hickel, Daniel W. O'Neill, Andrew L. Fanning, et al., 'National responsibility for ecological

breakdown: a fair-shares assessment of resource use, 1970–2017', *The Lancet Planetary Health*, 6(4), pp. e342–e349, 2022. For 92%, see Jason Hickel, 'Quantifying national responsibility for climate breakdown: an equality-based attribution approach for carbon dioxide emissions in excess of the planetary boundary', *The Lancet Planetary Health*, 4(9), pp. e399–e404, 2020.

12 Beatriz Rodríguez-Labajos, Ivonne Yánez, Patrick Bond, et al., 'Not so natural an alliance? Degrowth and environmental justice movements in the Global South', *Ecological Economics*, 157, pp. 175–184, 2019.

13 Sorcha Brennan, 'Kate Soper – The growth agenda is no longer feasible. What is the alternative?', Frontiers, 26 June 2023.

14 Corinna Dengler and Lisa Marie Seebacher, 'What about the Global South? Towards a feminist decolonial degrowth approach', *Ecological Economics*, 157(C), pp. 246–252, 2019.

15 Samuel Alexander, 'Life in a "degrowth" economy, and why you might actually enjoy it', The Conversation, 1 October 2014.

16 Howard Reed, Stewart Lansley, Matthew Johnson, et al., 'Tackling poverty: the power of a universal basic income', Compass: Basic Income Conversation, May 2022.

17 Juliet B. Schor, Wen Fan, Orla Kelly, et al., 'The four day week: assessing global trials of reduced work time with no reduction in pay', Four Day Week Global, 2022.

18 Andrew Simms, Anna Coote, Jane Franklin, '21 Hours: The case for a shorter working week', New Economics Foundation, 13 February 2010.

19 Zebras Unite, 'Zebras fix what unicorns break', Medium, 8 March 2017.

20 Ibid.

21 For 80%, see Guy Grainger, 'To create net-zero cities, we need to look hard at our older buildings', World Economic Forum,

8 November 2022. For 39%, see 'Bringing embodied carbon upfront', World Green Building Council, 2019.
22. Floor Kuitert, 'Can interspecies cohabitation open new doors for design?', *Frame*, 25 September 2023.
23. Circle Economy Foundation and Deloitte, 'The Circularity Gap Report 2024'.
24. Arthur Neslen, 'Extraction of raw materials to rise by 60% by 2060, says UN report', *The Guardian*, 31 January 2024.
25. Donella H. Meadows, *Thinking in Systems: A Primer* (Chelsea Green Publishing, 2008).
26. Luca Coscieme, Lewis Akenji, Elli Latva-Hakuni, et al., 'Unfit, unfair, unfashionable: resizing fashion for a fair consumption space', Hot or Cool Institute, 2022.
27. 'Attitudes towards single-use plastics', Ipsos and Plastic Free July, February 2022.
28. Emily Harris, Aleksander Nowak and Vlad Afanasiev, 'New economic thinking: enabling a just transition of the built environment in Europe', Dark Matter Labs and Laudes Foundation, 2022–2023.
29. Michael I. Norton, Daniel Mochon and Dan Ariely, 'The IKEA effect: when labor leads to love', *Journal of Consumer Psychology*, 22(3), pp. 453–460, July 2012.
30. 'The UK's "democratic economy" hits £87.9 billion as people turn to co-operatives and mutuals', Co-operatives UK, 27 September 2023.
31. Molly Liebergall, 'Author Talks: the world's longest study of adult development finds the key to happy living', McKinsey & Company, 16 February 2023.
32. Olamide Olaniyan, 'The most important climate action you can take? We asked Paul Hawken', The Tyee, 9 August 2021.
33. Chuck Collins, Omar Ocampo and Kalena Thomhave, 'High flyers 2023: how ultra-rich private jet travel costs the rest of us and burns up our planet', Patriotic Millionaires and The Institute for Policy Studies, May 2023.

34 'Latest air travel outlook reveals 2024 to be a milestone for global passenger traffic', Airports Council International World, 27 September 2023.
35 Stefan Gössling and Andreas Humpe, 'The global scale, distribution and growth of aviation: implications for climate change', *Global Environmental Change*, 65, November 2020.
36 Hiroko Tabuchi and Nadja Popovich, 'How guilty should you feel about flying?', *New York Times*, 17 October 2019.
37 Roger Harrabin, 'A few frequent flyers "dominate air travel"', BBC News, 31 March 2021.
38 Pierpaolo Cazzola, Leonardo Paoli and Jacob Teter, 'Trends in the global vehicle fleet 2023: managing the SUV shift and the EV transition', Global Fuel Economy Initiative, November 2023.
39 Jeremiah Budin, 'China's high-speed rail network just reached an incredible new milestone – will the rest of the world follow suit?', TCD Newsletter, 7 February 2024.
40 Jonathon Harker, 'German bike market quadruples in a decade to €7 billion', *Cycling Industry News*, 15 March 2023.
41 Kirsty Wild and Alistair Woodward, 'Why are cyclists the happiest commuters? Health, pleasure and the e-bike', *Journal of Transport & Health*, 14, September 2019.
42 Harald Schuster, Jolanda van der Noll and Anette Rohmann, 'Orientation towards the common good in cities: the role of individual urban mobility behavior', *Journal of Environmental Psychology*, 91, November 2023.

3. SOLARPUNK

1 Marjan van Aubel and Pauline van Dongen, 'The Solar Movement', October 2022.
2 Bryan Alexander, 'Solarpunk as a way of redesigning higher education for the climate crisis', Medium, 22 August 2023.
3 The Solarpunk Community, 'A Solarpunk Manifesto (English)', ReDes.

4 Adam Flynn, 'Solarpunk: notes toward a manifesto', Project Hieroglyph, 4 September 2014.
5 Ibid.
6 missolivialouise, Land of Masks and Jewels, Tumblr.
7 Justine Norton-Kertson, 'Solarpunk: giving off vibes – 2023 panel', *If This Goes On (Don't Panic): Science Fiction, Fantasy and Progressive Politics* podcast, 12 December 2023.
8 Adam Flynn, 'On the need for new futures', Solarpunks.net, 18 July 2012.
9 Rhys Williams, 'Solarpunk: against a shitty future', *Los Angeles Review of Books*, 10 March 2018.
10 Paul Graham Raven, 'The unbearable lightness of solarpunk', FoAM, 18 December 2022.
11 Connor Owens, 'What is solarpunk?', Solarpunk Anarchist, 27 May 2016.
12 *Sunvault: Stories of Solarpunk and Eco-Speculation* (Upper Rubber Boot Books, 2017) is credited as the first solarpunk anthology; *Solarpunk Magazine* was launched in 2022 with the tag line 'Demand Utopia'. Prominent solarpunk novels include Cory Doctorow's *The Lost Cause* (Head of Zeus – an AdAstra Book, 2023).
13 Alexandria Ocasio-Cortez (AOC), Instagram, 5 August 2023.
14 Krystal Persaud, 'Grist 50 2023: 50 climate leaders driving fresh solutions to our planet's biggest problems', Grist, September 2023.
15 Dave Jones et al., 'European Electricity Review 2023', Ember, 31 January 2023.
16 For 15.8%, see Lívia Neves, 'Brazil's solar capacity hits 34.9 GW, surpassing wind in national energy mix', *PV Magazine*, 1 December 2023. For 30%, see Susanna Twidale, 'Renewables provided record 30% of global electricity in 2023, Ember says', Reuters, 8 May 2024.
17 Colleen Howe, 'China's wind, solar capacity forecast to overtake coal in 2024', Reuters, 30 January 2024.

18 OpenNEM, Australia, 2024.
19 'Latest update on clean energy technology manufacturing shows a mixed outlook for key technologies', IEA, 24 November 2023.
20 Marjan van Aubel and Pauline van Dongen, 'The Solar Movement', October 2022.
21 Robert Rapier, 'Fossil fuels still account for 82% of primary global energy consumption', OilPrice.com, 10 August 2023.
22 Zachary Shahan, 'World needs to mine 25x more lithium by 2050', CleanTechnica, 20 October 2022.
23 Tega Brain, Alex Nathanson and Benedetta Piantella, 'Sun thinking', Solar Protocol.
24 Clare Farrell, Gail Bradbrook and Roger Hallam, 'Telling the truth so we can learn from our mistakes – reflections five years on', Extinction Rebellion, 19 October 2023.
25 Federica Zambeletti, 'The Great Endeavour: carbon removal infrastructure at a planetary scale', KoozArch, 23 June 2023.
26 Eric Hunting, 'Solarpunk: post-industrial design and aesthetics', Medium, 18 July 2020.
27 Jack Palfrey, 'Airships are back to clean up aviation. Will they take off?', *Positive News*, 24 May 2023.

4. METAVERSE

1 Keiichi Matsuda, speaking at 'Designing for New Realities', SXSW, 9 March 2024.
2 Matthew Ball, 'Framework for the metaverse', 29 June 2021.
3 Vernor Vinge, *True Names* (Dell Publishing, 1981).
4 William Gibson, 'Burning Chrome', *Omni*, July 1982.
5 Jillian D'Onfro, 'Facebook gives its Oculus employees a dystopian sci-fi book to get them excited about building the future', Business Insider, 27 July 2016.
6 'VPL Research Jaron Lanier', Virtual Reality Society.
7 Kayla Dowling, 'This immersive film explores how the metaverse will shape our domestic lives', *Frame*, 8 June 2022.

8 L.M. Sacasas, 'Too many words, and not enough', *The Convivial Society*, 4(6), 29 April 2023.
9 Konrad Putzier, 'Metaverse real estate piles up record sales in Sandbox and other virtual realms', *Wall Street Journal*, 30 November 2021.
10 Casey Newton, 'How Google is making up for lost time', *Platformer*, 11 May 2023.
11 Dave Karpf, 'On Jackpot Technologies, or, what Apple's new headset is actually *for*', *The Future, Now and Then*, 8 June 2023.
12 Hugo Barra, 'Vision Pro is an over-engineered "devkit" // Hardware bleeds genius & audacity but software story is disheartening // What we got wrong at Oculus that Apple got right // Why Meta could finally have its Android moment', Hugo's Blog, 11 March 2024.
13 'Taking Stock With Teens: Spring 2024 Survey', Piper Sandler, 4 September 2024.
14 Cara Aiello, Jiamei Bai, Jennifer Schmidt and Yurii Vilchynskyi, 'Probing reality and myth in the metaverse', McKinsey & Company, 13 June 2022.
15 Neil Shaw, 'We spend 75% of our waking hours glued to screens', *Manchester Evening News*, 28 October 2022.
16 Niccolo Soldo, 'The Dubrovnik Interviews: Marc Andreessen – interviewed by a retard', Fisted by Foucault, 31 May 2021.
17 Kathryn Y. Segovia and Jeremy N. Bailenson, 'Virtually true: children's acquisitions of false memories in virtual reality', *Media Psychology*, 12(4), November 2009.
18 Frank Steinicke and Gerd Bruder, 'A self-experimentation report about long-term use of fully-immersive technology', ACM Symposium on Spatial User Interaction (SUI), October 2014.
19 Jeremy N. Bailenson, Brian Beams, James Brown, et al., 'Seeing the world through digital prisms: psychological implications of passthrough video usage in mixed reality', *Technology, Mind, and Behavior*, 5(2) 2024.

20 'Cybersickness more likely to affect women, ongoing research to understand why', Iowa State University News Service, 2 May 2023.
21 'Survey of social VR users', PlutoVR and The Extended Mind, 27 March 2018.
22 Aisha Counts, 'VR headsets give enough data for AI to accurately guess ethnicity, income and more', Bloomberg, 10 August 2023.
23 Genevieve Bell, 'The metaverse is a new word for an old idea', *MIT Technology Review*, 8 February 2022.
24 Krista Kim, Instagram, 16 September 2022.
25 'My Self, My Avatar, My Identity: Diversity and Inclusivity Within Virtual Worlds', Institute of Digital Fashion, 2021.
26 Nick Yee, *The Proteus Paradox: How Online Games and Virtual Worlds Change Us – and How They Don't* (Yale University Press, 2014).
27 Patrick Barkham, 'People who work from home all the time "cut emissions by 54%" against those in office', *The Guardian*, 18 September 2023.
28 Eren Çam, Zoe Hungerford, Niklas Schoch, et al., 'Electricity 2024: analysis and forecast to 2026', IEA, 24 January 2024.
29 Keumars Afifi-Sabet, '"A mini data center village under the sea" – China sinks tens of thousands of powerful servers in fresh seawater as it grapples with demand for more power', TechRadar, 30 November 2023.
30 Magdalena M.H.E. van den Berg, Jolanda Maas, Rianne Muller, et al., 'Autonomic nervous system responses to viewing green and built settings: differentiating between sympathetic and parasympathetic activity', *International Journal of Environmental Research and Public Health*, 12(12), pp. 15860–15874, December 2015.
31 Kent Bye, '#600: Jaron Lanier's journey into VR: "Dawn of the new everything"', *Voices of VR* podcast, 5 December 2017.

Bibliography

Race After Technology: Abolitionist Tools for the New Jim Code, Ruha Benjamin (Polity, 2019)

Invisible Women: Exposing Data Bias in a World Designed for Men, Caroline Criado Perez (Vintage, 2019)

The Ministry for the Future, Kim Stanley Robinson (Orbit Books, 2020)

The Long Way to a Small, Angry Planet, Becky Chambers (Hodder & Stoughton, 2015)

A Psalm for the Wild-Built, Becky Chambers (St Martin's Press, 2021)

Copenhagen Institute for Futures Studies (https://cifs.dk)

The Spell of the Sensuous: Perception and Language in a More-Than-Human World, David Abram (Vintage Books, 1996)

An Immense World: How Animal Senses Reveal the Hidden Realms Around Us, Ed Yong (Bodley Head, 2022)

Pollinator Pathmaker, Alexandra Daisy Ginsberg (https://pollinator.art)

The Manifesto of Phyto-centred Design, Plant Fever (plantfever.com/The-Manifesto-of-Phyto-centred-Design)

AskNature, The Biomimicry Institute (https://asknature.org)

Black Faces, White Spaces: Reimagining the Relationship of African Americans to the Great Outdoors, Carolyn Finney (University of North Carolina Press, 2014)

Limits to Growth: The 30-Year Update, Donella H. Meadows, Jorgen Randers and Dennis Meadows (Chelsea Green, 2013)

The Economics of Arrival – Ideas for a Grown-Up Economy, Katherine Trebeck and Jeremy Williams (Policy Press, 2019)

Doughnut Economics: Seven Ways to Think Like a 21st-Century Economist, Kate Raworth (Random House, 2017)

Marx in the Anthropocene: Towards the Idea of Degrowth Communism, Kohei Saito (Cambridge University Press, 2023)

Thinking in Systems: A Primer, Donella H. Meadows (Chelsea Green Publishing, 2015)

A Bunch of Pretty Things I Did Not Buy, Sarah Lazarovic (Penguin Books, 2014)

BuyNothing (https://buynothingproject.org)

Transition Network (https://transitionnetwork.org)

The Solar Movement (https://thesolarmovement.org)

Solarpunks.net

Solarpunk: Ecological and Fantastic Stories in a Sustainable World, ed. Gerson Lodi-Ribeiro (World Weaver Press, 2018)

Solarpunk Magazine (https://solarpunkmagazine.com)

Instructables (https://www.instructables.com)

Run Your Own Social, Darius Kazemi (https://runyourown.social)

Solar Protocol (http://solarprotocol.net)

Incredible Edible Network (https://www.incredibleedible.org.uk)

Snow Crash, Neal Stephenson (Roc Books, 1992)

Ready Player One, Ernest Cline (Century, 2011)

Making a Metaverse That Matters, Wagner James Au (Wiley, 2023)

New World Notes (https://nwn.blogs.com)

'Burning Chrome', William Gibson (Orion, 2017)

Acknowledgements

This book is a work of synthesis. Thank you to the thinkers, makers, researchers and writers whose projects and ideas feature throughout; any misinterpretations are my own. I am grateful to the numerous people who gave me their time and insights while I was writing, including Jeremy Williams, Anab Jain, Adam Flynn, Jay Springett, Boudewijn Buitenhek, Lucy Hardcastle, Wagner James Au, Karinna Grant, Andreea Ion Cojocaru and Rachel Arthur.

My agent, Imogen Morrell, and publisher, Susie Nicklin, intuitively understood this book and energetically made it real.

WGSN was my professional home for more than a decade and is where I learned to be a trend forecaster, and how to assemble ideas and write clear and direct narratives. Many remarkable women inspired and guided me while I was there, particularly Lisa White and Helen Palmer, who infuse futures thinking with warmth, empathy and imagination.

My parents, Valerie and Norman Housley, raised me surrounded by books and ideas, and valuing the importance of both. Thank you.

My brilliant children, Eseld and Flynn, fill our days with energy and curiosity.

And thank you to Joe, who believed in this book from the very start and supported it and me unfailingly.

Transforming a manuscript into the book you hold in your hands is a group project.

Sarah Housley would like to thank everyone who helped to publish this book:

The Indigo Press Team

Susie Nicklin
Phoebe Barker
Phoebe Evans

Jacket Design

Luke Bird

Publicity

Sophie Portas

Editorial Production

Tetragon

Copy-editor

Jack Alexander

Proofreader

Sarah Terry

THE
INDIGO
PRESS

The Indigo Press is an independent publisher of contemporary fiction and non-fiction, based in London. Guided by a spirit of internationalism, feminism and social justice, we publish books to make readers see the world afresh, question their behaviour and beliefs, and imagine a better future.

Browse our books and sign up to our newsletter for special offers and discounts:

theindigopress.com

Follow *The Indigo Press* on social media for the latest news, events and more:

- ⓧ @PressIndigoThe
- ⓘ @TheIndigoPress
- ⓕ @TheIndigoPress
- ▣ The Indigo Press
- ⓙ @theindigopress